The Original Chicago Hauntings Companion

Ursula Bielski

AMERICAN GHOST BOOKS

Cover Illustrations by Anna Huffman
Printed in the United States of America
ISBN: 979-8-9915482-3-6

CONTENTS

GHOSTS OF CHECAGOU 1

GHOSTS OF THE GREAT FIRE 9

GHOSTS OF LINCOLN PARK 19

THE HANCOCK CENTER 35

CURSE OF THE CORN COBS 41

THE TRIBUNE TOWER 45

THE FIELD MUSEUM 49

THE DEVIL BABY OF HULL HOUSE 53

THE ST. VALENTINE'S DAY MASSACRE 61

THE BIOGRAPH THEATER 67

THE CONGRESS PLAZA 75

DEATH'S ALLEY 83

THE EASTLAND DISASTER 91

RESURRECTION MARY 95

ABOUT THE AUTHOR 111

GHOSTS OF CHECAGOU

In Chicago's South Loop neighborhood, a little park rests between the new, expensive condominium complexes along Calumet Avenue, where 18th street cuts from Indiana Avenue East to the Lake, skirting the stately Prairie Avenue historic district. It is a strangely small patch of grass, but with a historic marker designating it as one of the most important sites in the city's history. But before the bronze marker was forged, a much different, much older monument stood: an ancient cottonwood known for generations as the "Massacre Tree." The Tree was believed by many to have marked ground zero of the gruesome Fort Dearborn Massacre of 1812, a defining moment in Chicago's memory, and one of the most truly haunting in American history.[2]

---

1 The Massacre Tree at Prairie Avenue in what is today's South Loop, near Soldier Field. (Chicago Public Library)

2 For years, this monument commemorating the Fort Dearborn Massacre stood on Prairie Avenue. (Library of Congress)

In the summer of 1812, the settlement at Fort Dearborn was young, diverse, and fatally unstable, comprised, in the words of Nelson Algren, of "Yankee and voyageur, the Irish and the Dutch, Indian traders and Indian agents, half breed and quarter breed and no breed at all."[3] The place was known as Checagou by the Native Americans. It was their name for the wild onions that grew here in profusion in 1800. By then, the competition for hunting areas and trade routes had ruined much of the independence natural to the Great Lakes tribes. The native element of the emergent pan-Indian culture could not avoid engaging in trade-based subsistence and became largely dependent on trade goods. Their pottery making had become extremely rare by 1780, and the cultivation of maize, once a unifying tribal activity, had devolved into a means of supporting white populations. Soon, the inevitable depletion of wild game forced the Potawatomi to repurchase their own harvests from white traders. The toppling of the Chicago area's native equilibrium happened in the blink of an eye. Jean Baptiste Point Du Sable, a mixed-race fur trader from Santo Domingo, had been the area's first settler, living at the river for 20 years before the turn of the 19th century. During his residence there, the wilderness had remained literally unbroken. After living peaceably in a modest home for nearly two decades, Du Sable sold his land to a man named John Lalime, who aimed to take up indefinite residence in Du Sable's quiet cabin at the mouth of the river. That intention was abruptly halted when John Kinzie arrived in Chicago and seized the property in 1803. Although the Kinzie title has still not been found, most historians agreed that the house, on the bank of the Chicago River opposite the fort, was the same lot that Du Sable sold to Lalime in 1800. Records in Detroit, however, show the sale of that same land to Kinzie by Pierre Menard, who passed the parcel to Kinzie for fifty dollars, claiming to have purchased it from an Indian named Bonhomme. When Kinzie arrived in Chicago, he assumed the right to the disputed title, at the same time beginning a rivalry with Lalime that would end in the murder of the latter at the hands of his foe.

Yet, only with Kinzie's whirlwind arrival, less than a decade before the fort's destruction, did the settlement at the river begin to come alive. Preceded by his reputation as a quick-witted Indian trader, Kinzie, a British subject born in Detroit's Grosse Pointe area, immediately settled his family in the safe shadow of Fort Dearborn.

---

3   Nelson Algren, "City on the Make"

For nearly ten years, he ruled the realm of settlers and "savages" that together began to suggest civilization, at least when Kinzie himself wasn't sparring with his fellows. For Kinzie was a melding of opportunism and temerity, and when he came to Chicago, aiming to position himself between the portage fur trappers and the Detroit market, he brought along his whole collection of brash personality traits to help him along, using what one critic called "guile, intimidation, and the soporific effects of British rum" to "persuade" Detroit bound trappers to undersell him their pelts.

Kinzie's attitude set the standard for the business relationships that affected every aspect of life at Fort Dearborn. That attitude took its life largely from the shared distaste of men like Kinzie for all others, something that overshadowed any feelings of community.

Still, Kinzie's self-assuredness served to comfort and encourage those who sensed in him a certain quality of leadership. And it was this self-styled security enjoyed by Kinzie and his comrades that left them ill-prepared for the events to come. Eventually, the resentment of the native population became too strong for even a charmer like Kinzie to dismiss.

The inevitable slap of reality came in 1812 when fighting erupted along the northwestern frontier. The fate of more than the fort was sealed when a pair of decisions was delivered. General Hull's order of the evacuation of the fort was quickly followed by Captain Nathan Heald's own demand that the settlers and soldiers destroy all whiskey and gunpowder—a decision that enraged the Native Americans.

On August 15, 1812, Captain Billy Wells arrived at Fort Dearborn, escorted by friendly Miami Indians from his home of Fort Wayne, Indiana. His plan was to give the hostile Natives at Fort Dearborn everything his band could carry, in hopes that the Indians would allow the Fort Dearborn settlers safe passage across the dunes to Fort Wayne. But while Wells had a plan, he didn't have a hope: he arrived at the Fort that morning with black paint smeared over his face: a sign he believed his death would come before day's end.

Predictably, as the grim procession of soldiers and settlers crossed into the open landscape headed toward Indiana, Indian allies of the British beheld them with bitter eyes. When the line reached a smattering of cottonwood saplings near present day 18th Street and Indiana Avenue, a group of Potawatomi pounced.

Of the 148 members of the exodus, 86 men and women and 12 children were brutally scalped and murdered, a wagon of children axed in their skulls (claimed by the Indians to have been an act of mercy because their parents had been killed). Billy Wells fell with the dead, and the Indians promptly cut out his heart and ate it to absorb his immense courage.

Those who survived were taken as prisoners. Some of these died soon after, while others were enslaved and later sold to the British and into freedom.

Appealing to the Potawatomi on the strength of the business relationships that he had forged, Kinzie and his family were spared.

The fort was burned down.

The scalped corpses of victims remained unburied where they fell, splayed across the Lake Michigan dunes or half buried in the loamy soil. When troops began arriving four years later, they were met by a ghastly host of images: the pitiful skeleton of the erstwhile fort; the abandoned Kinzie cabin; the decaying bodies of settlers and soldiers, all returned to the prairie, all victims of the wilderness and of a desperate, undeclared war.

By the time John Kinzie returned to his property a year later, troops erecting the new Fort Dearborn had re-buried many of Kinzie's neighbors in the new fort's cemetery. Never looking back, Kinzie sought in vain to climb again to his old seat at the peak of the portage fur trade. When his bitter efforts went unsatisfied, he stooped to employment with the new king, the American Fur Company.

The gruesome events that occurred on the Chicago dunes that summer day in 1812 seem to demand commemoration via haunting legends. Indeed, the site of the fort itself is reported to be well-protected by marching troops of massacred soldiers who stand guard over the phantom fort site, now the south end of the Michigan Avenue bridge. Yet the site of the actual massacre remained placid until many decades later, after the physical formation of the city of Chicago. Only then, during routine roadwork near the site, did workers uncover remains dating to the early 1800s which were probably massacre victims.

Whatever the identity of the remains, after the accidental excavation, apparitions described as "settlers" began to present themselves to passers-by near 18th and Calumet.

Today, the site of the Fort Dearborn Massacre is barely distinguishable as the place where, over two centuries ago, an iconic scene played out on the bloodied sands of the fledgling *Checagou*. A handful of the old mansions still stand along cobblestoned Prairie Avenue, most of them demolished and rebuilt, ironically, "in the fashion of" the destroyed houses.

And what houses they were.

For years after the Great Fire, Prairie Avenue was Chicago's "easy street," where the wealthiest of the city's movers and shakers made their homes. But while the digs were unrivaled as the century turned, in short order the avenue fell into darkness and decline, affected by the busy Illinois Central railroad tracks immediately east and, much worse, the nearby Levee vice district in present-day Chinatown.

After the exodus, only a half dozen of almost one hundred of the mansions here were left standing.

Behind the door of 1800 South Prairie Avenue, the John Glessner House retains all of the vitality envisioned for it by its architect, Henry Hobson Richardson. The house, with its Arts and Crafts feel a harbinger of the great architects to come, was popularly believed to have been Richardson's last commission. In July 1885, however, more than a year after the plans were drawn up for Glessner House, Frank Mac Veagh, who would later become secretary of the treasury of the United States, requested that Richardson design a home at 1220 North Lake Shore Drive. The architect agreed and went on to witness the completion of his design for a lakefront Romanesque brownstone after that of Glessner House.

According to Glessner's accounts, Richardson toured the lots at south Prairie Avenue and Eighteenth Street and drew up the sketches for the house the very next day. Glessner, loving the house as much as the architect did, wrote a book for his children about his time there. Through its doors, the elite of Chicago came and went, as they did through many thresholds on this fabled street. Glessner was not Henry Richardson's last creative gesture, but to him and the majority of his peer architects, it was the pinnacle of his genius.

It should not be surprising then that this is where Richardson's spirit is rumored to linger. For years, inhabitants have identified their unseen border as the house's designer and not its owner. The giveaway is the manner in which he manifests: to visitors touring the house, who are delighted by their docent's intense understanding of and love for the house's architectural nuances. Often, when these same guests comment to the house staff on their charming guide, they are informed that no guides were on duty that day—their tour was given by a ghost.

While Richardson walks the rooms of Glessner House, his ghost is not alone on this storied street. Phantoms are said to still hover around the old Clarke House, situated in a small park in the center of the block. Tales of phantom horses are told by strollers, their clip clopping echoing on the cobblestones, and now and then a woman in settler's dress flits from bush to flower in the moonlight before vanishing in the mist. The Clarke House is a much older house than the Prairie Avenue mansions, as it was moved from its original location on the Chicago prairie. It was thought to be the oldest house in Chicago until Norwood Park's Seymour Noble-Crippen House was found to have an earlier pedigree.

The Kimball mansion still stands on the southeast corner of Eighteenth and Prairie, across from Glessner House. Built for the founder of Chicago's famed organ manufacturing company, the house is both stately and supernatural. Behind its doors walks the ghost of Evaline Kimball, the music magnate's wife, who has been known to rattle the windows at all hours of the day and night for nearly a century.

The mammoth doors of the Elbridge Keith mansion are often visited by guests to magnificent weddings and other events still held here. In between sips and dances, they sometimes encounter an invisible attendee or two. In fact, during one paranormal-themed event, three separate mediums claimed to sense strong spirits in many corners of the rooms.

All other houses on Prairie Avenue—enduring or demolished—pale, however, in comparison to the thirty-thousand-square-foot fortress of Marshall Field Jr., which has been converted in recent years into six luxury condominiums. The building was used as a hospital and as a nursing home, among other things, since its abandonment during the street's decay. But at least one resident stayed behind: the house's namesake.

Field Jr.—son of Chicago's department store king—was reportedly given the house as a wedding gift by his father. The house, however, proved to be much bigger than the groom's vows. When he was found shot to death in a bedroom of the house in the fall of 1905, rumor had it that he had been involved with a woman from the notorious Everleigh Club brothel in the Levee district nearby. Though the shooting was explained by the family as an accident that occurred while Field Jr. was cleaning a hunting rifle, it was whispered that he had been shot at the club and then carried home under cover of darkness and silence. Left behind were a widow and three young children, who deserted the house, never to return.

Modern owners of the main front unit today talk about a filmy figure of a man seen and heard pacing the halls and treading the stairs regularly—an entity believed by most to be that of the tragic figure of Field.

GHOSTS OF THE GREAT FIRE

4

In his "Five Months After" essay, which appeared in the Chicago Times in April 1872, editor Everett Chamberlain reiterated an American joke that had been enjoyed in recent months, especially by Chicagoans: the joke wherein a citizen of some far-off town was represented as rushing with mad haste to the railway station…because, as he said, he must reach Chicago…or they would have the whole town built up again before he could get a view of the ruins.[5]

And it was true.

The swift, phoenix-like emergence of the post-fire city—stronger, bigger, better than before—gained Chicago a permanent and worldwide reputation as an unstoppable metropolis: "The City that Works." Yet, while Chicagoans quickly dismissed the disaster in favor of the future, the first few days after the Great Conflagration found Chicagoans filled with despair and the nation and world desperate for details.

Full of the monstrous news and eager for sympathetic ears, stunned Chicagoans wrote to friends and relations around the world, sending much-anticipated news of the state of the city. Without photos or newsreels to provide a vision of the disaster, out-of-towners relied on the vivid descriptions of the fire's own witnesses. Chicagoans' letters

---

4   The Water Tower circa 1930 (Library of Congress)

5   Everett Chamberlain, "Five Months After," *The Lakeside Monthly*, vol. 7 (April 1872): 314.

regarding the disaster remain some of the city's most precious historical resources, providing as they do keen and colorful witness to the great conflagration. Many of these letters' authors document their own destruction, tracing in a rush of words their overnight falls from wealth and luxury to impoverished homelessness. The loss of family and of friends. Others, luckier, report on the misfortune of others.[6]

Anna Higginson, wife of George M. Higginson, real estate broker, lived with her husband on Dearborn Street, just north of Chicago Avenue. While the city still smoldered, she sent word of the fire to her friend, Mrs. Mark Skinner, in Europe with her husband at the time, including literary pictures of the fire's attendant madness:

> *Mrs. Winston saved a pink silk dress trimmed with lace, but very little else; one lady had a carriage full of party dresses & another a half dozen bonnets. One man was seen running from the fire with two immense turnips & another with a piece of broken furniture.*

But while these snapshots peppered the city's memory in the days after the fire, most of the lasting remembrance was vivid film, destined to replay itself forever in the city's mind:

> *(T)he fire worked up gradually along the North Branch & the instant the wind caught it the fire was hurled the whole length of the city; in that way our house was burned at last. As I went out of it & saw the vine-covered walls & the windows filled with flowers all shining so peacefully in the moonlight, it seemed impossible to realize that in a few moments the smoke & flame I saw all around me would seize that too & that I was looking upon my home for the last time.*

This destitution would be, for most, a temporary condition, yet an unquestionable blanket of loss was fixed forever. As the once formidable temples to commerce, trade, worship and art—wonders of the modern world—lay in ruins around him, the Mayor of Chicago had but one desolate dispatch to the nation:

---

6 Excerpts in this section are from the Chicago Historical Society's *The Great Chicago Fire.*

Send us food for the suffering. Our city is in ashes.

Incredibly, the unspeakable destruction left behind by the "memorable conflagration" written of by Chamberlain five months after the fire was not exclusively attributable to the fire itself. In fact, a significant portion of the damage was the work of looters and thieves, who took advantage of the chaos and the preoccupation of police forces to plunder the burning city.

"The like of this sight since Sodom & Gomorra [*sic*] has never met human vision," wrote Jonas Hutchinson, lawyer and notary. "No pen can tell what a ruin this is." But he tried. To his mother in New Hampshire, Hutchinson penned his own testimony of the fire and the blackness that described far more than its charred ruins:

> *(T)he city is thronged with desperadoes who are plundering & trying to set new fires. The police are vigilant. Thousands of special police are on duty. Every block has its patrolmen and instructions are explicit to each officer to shoot any man who acts suspicious and will not answer when spoken to the second time. Several were shot & others hung to lamp posts last night under these instructions....The roughs are improving the time to sack & pillage. The city is in darkness.*

When I first studied the ghost stories of the Great Fire many years ago, I wrote: "Least evident here today is the lawlessness of autumn, 1871, when looters swung from the lampposts, desperately subdued by attempts at law and order during a reign of absolute terror." But times are different now. Current newspapers now regularly carry stories of the "wilding" carried out by gangs of youths assaulting random tourists and locals in this historic district and throughout the central part of the city. As the world knows, chaos has returned to Chicago, and it is an everyday chaos.

But our history remains, with its own ghosts. Just as the Water Tower itself forces the fire's memory on all who pass its castellated remains, so too do some of the players in that drama. In an upper window of the old tower, before its renovation and even now, passersby have occasionally seen the figure of a man, limp and pallid, dangling by a rope around his neck, or sitting quietly, staring from the window. Workers in the information center profess ignorance of the sightings, testifying that memory alone haunts this structure.

On October 21, 1875, a young man named Frederick Kaiser had lunch with his family in their home on Pearson Street. He usually sat and read with his family after lunch, but that day he said he was going out for a walk. He crossed the street, climbed to the top of the water tower and sat for some time looking out of the window, where numerous passersby saw him. At about half past two o'clock, he jumped.[7]

In June 1881, a young shop clerk named Hugo von Malapert jumped too.[8]

Today, many historians claim that the execution of the Great Fire's looters is a myth. Accidental deaths did occur, of course, in the course of law enforcement. But the wide-scale and officially approved hanging of criminals is, many say, the stuff of legend.

Still, the letters remain, their authors' descriptions of the hangings as vivid now as ever. And even those who disregard them may someday catch a glimpse of the proof they need: one hapless witness to the rule that crime doesn't pay, paying his own dues forever in the city's signature tower.

A much more heartwarming story of the fire is also one of the city's most beloved: the legend of Fr. Arnold Damen and his "deal with God" on that terrible night in 1871.

Extending skyward from the corner of Roosevelt Road and May Street on the city's south side is the impressive spire of Holy Family Church, the centerpiece of one of Chicago's oldest Catholic parishes and a seemingly indestructible monument to the unmoving faith of its ever-changing congregation.

Erected in 1857 as the core of a Jesuit-guided parish, Holy Family Church was, according to folklorist Richard Crowe, built over the site of an Indian battlefield, and, incidentally, over the running waters of the Red Creek. When the Chicago Fire failed to destroy the church just

---

7   "Self-Destruction," *Chicago Tribune*, October 22, 1875, 8.
8   "A Sensational Suicide," *Wayne County Herald*, June 23, 1881, 2.

14 years after its completion, the parishioners attributed the apparent miracle to the intervention of Our Lady of Perpetual Help.

The night of the fire, the parish's founder, Father Arnold Damen, was in New York City doing missionary work. Hearing confessions at Brooklyn's St. Patrick's Church, another priest passed a note to Damen in the confessional, telling him that Chicago was aflame and his parish in the direct line of its destruction.

Father Damen quietly finished hearing confessions then walked up to the altar. He knelt down and prayed, staying on his knees the whole night through. He prayed for the intercession of the Blessed Mother, Our Lady of Perpetual Help. He promised the Blessed Mother that if God would save his parish, he would build a shrine to her honor at Holy Family and keep seven candles burning there forever.

Back in Chicago, as the Fire raged through the city, it seemed intent on ravishing Fr. Damen's parish and the homes of his flock. But then, something extraordinary happened. The wind changed without warning, and the flames skirted the Near West side neighborhood while Damen's parishioners waited with bated breath, on their knees too, inside the church Fr. Damen had built. After the Fire, the shrine was built. Today, seven (now electric) candles still blaze at all hours of the day and night, the kept promise of the faithful Fr. Damen.

Fr. Damen was one of a dozen Belgian Jesuit missionaries who was brought to America by the Jesuit missionary to the American Indians, Father Pierre-Jean De Smet. Like his brothers, Damen first went to Florissant, Missouri, just outside St. Louis, living at the Jesuit monastery of St. Stanislaus. He was ordained in 1843, three years after his arrival in the United States, and his first assignment was as a parish priest in the city.

In the summer of 1856, while Fr. Damen served as pastor of Saint Francis Zavier Parish in St. Louis, he traveled to Chicago to preach a string of missions. The missions were an overwhelming success, leading Chicago's Bishop O'Regan to invite the Missouri Jesuits to establish a parish in Chicago, where the Order had no existing community. That fall, O'Regan wrote to Damen in St. Louis, urging the project:

I know I cannot do a better work for religion, for the diocese or for my own soul than by establishing here a house of your Society, and this is the reason I have been so very anxious to effect this. It was on this account, as also from my personal regard and affection for your Institute, as for many of your Fathers individually, that I so urgently and perseveringly tried to see this good work accomplished.

The church building which Fr. Damen erected is something of a miracle in itself. No one could quite understand how this massive and exquisite structure had risen from literally nothing, as Fr. Damen's parishioners were the poorest of the poor and most of the funds for construction he had to raise on his own. The secret was Damen's charisma: a magical power which compelled hundreds to give literal nickels and dimes from their scant incomes—and caused the occasional wealthy neighbor to hand over great sums of money at Fr. Damen's request. For his love of the Church—and particularly of his church—was contagious. Soon, the parish of the Holy Family was the pride and joy of thousands: a shining oasis of faith and hope in Chicago's West side ghetto.

The familiar robes of the Jesuit can be found on various the men portrayed in the statues displayed at Holy Family: many of the saints venerated here are the brother men who inspired and worked with Fr. Damen. A curious addition to these is a pair of wooden statues depicting two altar boys in old-fashioned cassocks. The statues immortalize two youngsters who have played leading roles in the mysterious history of this spiritual community. Indelibly etched in parish memory is the story of the tragedy that befell the two brothers when they were drowned together in 1863 and of their subsequent appearances to fellow parishioners, a story repeated by Father David McCarthy during his time at Holy Family parish. McCarthy told the late Chicago folklorist Richard Crowe that he had verified the drownings through parish records, though to date no names or details of the tragedy have been publicly revealed.

In 1890, Fr. Damen was awakened by what was later believed to be the deceased brothers. Dressed in cassocks and bearing lighted candles, the children led the priest to the dying mother of the departed boys, then promptly vanished. Along with this original account, later parish legends developed around the story. Some reports hold that even several years before their deaths, phantasms of the boys appeared to would be victims of the Chicago Fire to warn these parishioners of their imminent danger. But while the presence of the boys has faded in recent generations, that of Fr. Darnen has been infused with greater energy than ever.

But if Arnold Damen was always there for his church and his flock, protecting both from earthly, and netherworldly, harm, it was his beloved school that won his undying passion. St. Ignatius College Prep is an anomaly, a school unmatched for Chicago prestige, but open through scholarship to the super-rich, the dirt-poor, and everyone in between. The result is a student body that's an education in itself; those lucky and smart enough to gain admission live daily with a cross-section of society, forming friendships with young people from Hyde Park to Homewood, Bronzeville to Beverly, Garfield Park to the Gold Coast. St. Ignatius alums, then, are among the most sophisticated and successful of all Chicagoans. Fr. Damen would be proud. During his lifetime, the Jesuit strove for the school's superiority in all things: the curriculum, the culture, and, most notably, the spiritual life of the students it served. Some say that, after his death, Damen continued to serve as the school's headmaster of sorts, overseeing the campus in his usual, ever-loving way. Along with the well-being of the students, he keeps close watch on the physical property, ensuring that all is in tip-top shape and that Ignatius's future is secure.

When, in the early 1980s, the board initiated a massive renovation for the century-old school, elaborate plans were drawn up for the near-gutting of most of the structure, an updating of all the electrical and plumbing systems, and the installation of new floors and ceilings where water damage and wear had taken its toll. As with all such projects, a director was assigned to oversee the remodeling through to its completion. Not on the payroll, however, was another far more authoritative boss: Arnold Damen, the project's self-appointed foreman.

Since the founder's death, a number of students and faculty had spotted Damen casually patrolling the halls of Ignatius, going about his rounds as he always had, but by the dawn of the 1980s, sightings of him had all but ended. With the beginning of renovation Damen reappeared with a vengeance, startling those witnesses unschooled in his legacy.

One 1985 graduate tells the story of his own run-in with the ghost of Damen during an after-hours pledge drive for the renovation-in-progress:

In the mid-1980s, the school began a fundraising campaign to raise money for badly needed repairs to the school. Some of the urgent work had already begun replacing rotten flooring and tuckpointing. Students would work late into the night on this project, calling former students to raise money for the campaign. The calling center was set up in an old, musty library on the top floor of the school, known then as the Cambridge Room. It was a dark and dreary place, with old, dusty books and sheets of plastic covering the windows. Outside employees who had been hired to manage the campaign often times worked late, too (past midnight), preparing letters and managing the records. They often felt strange sensations, like another person was in the room with them, when there were only two employees in the building. The school had a very sophisticated alarm system installed, since it was in a very bad area of the city, and several times this alarm went off while the fundraising campaign was being conducted—the keypad had an LCD display that would ominously flash the word "Intruder" when the alarm went off. Though the system had been in place for several years it had never before experienced a false alarm, so every time the alarm would go off the Chicago police would respond with canine teams, and the school would be searched, with negative results. There were never any indications of forcible entry, and everything was always found locked and secured.

One night, I was standing in the library talking to one of the management people, when I glanced through the set of large, old wooden doors that led to an unused hallway. The hallway also served as a foyer for two old, curved stairways, an old elevator, and a large storeroom. I watched an old man about five-foot, six-inches tall and very thin, with white hair, balding, extremely pale, and dressed all in black clothing (a long-sleeved black shirt and long slacks). The person moved very quickly and lightly on a diagonal across the wide hallway, and it was odd, since the floors were very old wood and creaked badly; even so, no sound was made by this man I saw.

I said to the manager, 'There is someone in the building,' and I pointed out to the hallway and told him what I'd seen. He told the other manager, and they were concerned and went to investigate. As the stairwell was closed off and the elevators not in service, the only place the old man could have gone was into the storeroom on the south side of the hallway. The room was, surprisingly, locked, and when the manager unlocked the door, we found that the floor and ceiling of the room had already been removed by construction crews working on the renovations. We looked down nearly twenty feet to the classroom below and up nearly twenty feet into the pitch-black ceiling of the attic of the school.

We were terrified. A hasty meeting was called, and the students were sent home several hours early. The managers—who had, of course, had their own experiences in the building— left with us, and no one was willing to look through the upper floors of the school that night, or to call the police, who had come in vain more than once before to apprehend "intruders" who couldn't be found.

Later, when I told older priests at the school what I'd seen, there was no question in their minds that I'd seen Fr. Damen, the founder of the school, to whom the physical maintenance of the building had always been of the utmost importance. Although I knew well of Damen, as he occupied the most prominent of places in the school's proud history, I had never heard the stories of his haunting of the place. Still, everyone I spoke to who knew of the priest's ghost asserted at once that he had likely come back—as he had many times before—this time to keep an eye on the renovations.

Aside from his love for Holy Family and St. Ignatius—seemingly defying the grave—there may be another reason for Fr. Damen's lingering presence. After his death, he was interred in the cemetery on the grounds of St. Stanislaus Seminary in Florissant, Missouri—where Damen had first arrived so many years before as a young missionary monk before his ordination. And where the bodies of his brother missionaries (including Fr. DeSmet) also rested. In recent years, after the closure and sale of the Seminary to a Christian school, the bodies of the Jesuits who had been laid to rest there were slated to be moved to Calvary Cemetery in St. Louis. In a story that seems a broken record now, bystanders during the days of the removals claim that no remains were removed—only the headstones. When pressed, authorities insisted that whatever remains were still present were indeed reinterred—but that there was not much to be found after so many years.

Today, visitors make their way to the memorial site of the Belgian missionaries in St. Louis, but are the remains of these great missionaries really here?

Ghostly goings-on at the old Seminary grounds since the "re-interments" in Florissant seem to question the official record, as paranormal investigation teams have made this a regular point of pilgrimage on their evening outings. Strange lights, shadowy figures and even the sounds of chant are experienced on the site of the old cemetery at St. Stanislaus, causing one to wonder about the wanderings—after death—of at least one of the old faithful.

GHOSTS OF LINCOLN PARK

Though the ghosts of Lincoln Park get their own chapter, a great number of them are also ghosts of the Great Fire as well.

Before the establishment of City Cemetery, Chicago had made some poor decisions concerning the question of burial. The area's first homesteaders along the river had buried their kin in their backyards, leading to a few surprises later on when the downtown area was dug up to lay the foundations for skyscrapers and other developments. In addition, the Chicago River sometimes played tricks on the bereaved who might bid farewell to their loved ones only to watch them floating by on the waterway sometime later, having been purged from their graves after a particularly heavy rain. Further, the two cemeteries that were finally established in 1835—a Protestant one at Chicago and Michigan avenues and a Catholic one near 23rd Street and Calumet Avenue—were both situated squarely on the lake shore, leading to the frequent unearthing of caskets. When population increases added to the inadequacy of the funerary system, the city selected acreage at Clark Street and North Avenue on which to found Chicago City Cemetery. Simultaneously, the Roman Catholic Diocese of Chicago secured for its faithful a portion of property between Dearborn and State streets, south of North Avenue. Though none of this land was exactly towering above the water table, any of it was preferable to the shaky sepulchers of the earliest burial grounds. The transfer of bodies to the new sites began at once.

9   The Couch Tomb in Lincoln Park (Library of Congress)

Scarcely a decade after the opening of the new cemeteries, however, Chicagoans began to loudly complain about them. Besides the overcrowding resulting from both population growth and a string of cholera epidemics, echoes of earlier days could be heard in the fear that inadequate burials were leading to increased disease and contamination of the water. Fueling this near panic was the fact that the city morgue, as well as a holding building for epidemic victims, (the so-called Pest House), were both located on the Chicago City Cemetery grounds. By the mid- 1850s, concerned congregations and families were beginning to bury their loved ones at "safer," outlying sites such as Graceland, Rosehill, Calvary, and Oak Woods.

By the early 1870s, City Cemetery was closed. Then began the long process of removal of the thousands of graves already in place.

Some didn't go quietly.

It seems that nearly every Chicagoan, and many a tourist for that matter, is aware that native businessman Ira Couch (1806–1857) is dead, though almost no one knows exactly who he was, what he did, or why his tomb stands in the middle of Lincoln Park. For generations, drivers along the park's rich sweep of green have ogled the hotelkeeper and realtor's somber tomb with a mixture of keen curiosity and frank unease, wondering at the explanation for this odd ornament affixed in the backyard of the Chicago History Museum. When the mass evacuation began, the Couch family reportedly rallied and appealed to officials to let the tomb remain due to the cost of transporting the mausoleum to another site. In time, the city consented, and so the Couch tomb remains, though many historians believe that Ira Couch is actually interred in Rosehill Cemetery, along with the rest of the clan.

Another famous "removal" from City Cemetery was that of little Inez Clarke, who went on to become one of the city's most famous ghosts after her reinterment at Graceland Cemetery, a bit north up Clark Street, just past Wrigley Field. Her story has been ruthlessly and regularly dismembered for two decades by a long line of historians and journalists, but I think it's finally been permanently put back together.

Struck down in her girlhood by either tuberculosis or a lightning bolt (the versions of the tale often differ), the story goes that Inez was buried in Graceland by her devastated parents, who proceeded to commission a statue of their lost angel for her gravesite. That monument, perhaps the most affecting of any Chicago child's, depicts the little lady in her favorite dress, perched on a wooden chair and holding a dainty parasol. Her gleaming eyes hover above a whisper of a smile. Surrounding the masterpiece is a box made of glass, securely cemented to the monument's base.

Years ago, reports began to circulate that the statue had come up missing one night, only to be found in place the next morning. Apparently, this happened on several occasions until, according to the story, the glass case was placed over the monument to prevent further theft. When a security guard making his rounds discovered the empty case one night, despite it being securely anchored to the base, he fled the cemetery at once, leaving the grounds unattended and the gates standing open.

Accounts differ as to whether Inez's statue began disappearing before or after her monument was encased in glass. Those who attest to her death by lightning say that she only disappears during violent storms, perhaps seeking shelter from the frightening weather, while those who credit her death to tuberculosis say that she runs off at random. Occasionally, a visitor will claim to have seen a child who wanders and disappears among the graves near the Clarke monument, and stories tell of children visiting the cemetery with their families and wander off, only to be found near the statue, uttering claims that they were "playing with Inez."

Cemetery records do indicate that a child was buried in that spot in August 1880, but that the child's name was Amos Briggs. No "Inez Clarke" exists in Graceland's records at all.

In 2009, Chicago historian John Binder got to the bottom of the confusing mystery behind Graceland's most famous ghost. The Inez who was buried here was Inez Briggs, who died of diphtheria at the age of six, in August 1880. Her death certificate specifies Graceland as the intended burial site. Binder theorized that the names "Inez" and "Amos" had been mixed up in the cemetery record. He found that at the time of her death, Inez was living with her mother, Mary McClure, and her grandparents David and Jane Rothrock in what is now the 800 block of West Armitage Avenue. By 1872, Inez's father, Walter Briggs, was gone and Mary wed John Clarke. Though Inez was not his daughter, the family had that carved on her tombstone, leading to almost a century and a half of mystery.[10]

Though the mystery of Inez's name has been solved, her ghost has not been laid to rest. She still wanders Graceland Cemetery on stormy nights here, defying all who call her a fairy tale.

After all the unpleasant lessons had been learned, Chicago went about its business, secure in the belief that Lincoln Park's posh property was virtually corpse-free, except for the tomb of Mr. Couch and the unmarked grave of David Kennison (1736—1852), who claimed to be a 116-year-old Boston Tea Party survivor. But a far different story would someday come to light, after smoldering for generations just under the surface.

During an interview with researcher Pamela Bannos around the year 2000, Lester Fisher, erstwhile director of Lincoln Park Zoo, (which stands on the old cemetery property), talked of a casket being found in 1962 when the foundation was dug for the familiar red barn at the "Farm in the Zoo" exhibit on the Zoo's wWest end. When the City gave no response to requests for direction for dealing with the remains, Zoo administration directed the reburial of the remains where they had been found. The remains were reinterred, concrete was poured, and the barn built on top, where it stands (and where the remains lie) today.

In 1970, bones were found during the building of an addition to the Chicago Historical Society, (today the Chicago History Museum), at North Avenue and Clark Street. Then, again, in 1998 the remains of 81 corpses were discovered during excavation for the museum's parking lot, just north of the La Salle Street extension to Lake Shore Drive.

Adhering to the Human Skeletal Remains Protection Act, an archaeologist was contacted to work with the Museum on a proper excavation of the remains. Archaeologist David Keene found bone fragments in initial soil samples of the area, and so the Illinois Historic Preservation Agency

---

10   Mark Konkol, "Ghost Story Back from the Dead," *Chicago Sun-Times*, October 30, 2009.

blessed the excavation project with a permit. The excavated were sent to the collections of the Illinois State Museum in Springfield and painstakingly catalogued. The only partial corpses, which all were only partial, were found to belong to 81 different individuals. Along with the skeletons discovered, Keene's team also uncovered a Fisk metallic burial case with a corpse inside.

One of the central reasons for the prevalence of abandoned graves was the destruction of markers in the Great Fire of 1871. At that time, many grave markers were made of wood, (called "headboards."), and history abounds with stories of panicked Chicagoans seeking refuge from the fire in the open graves of the slowly transitioning property, carrying with them their scant but cherished property, which was yet eventually abandoned to the flames.

In *The Great Conflagration*, written immediately after the Fire, James W. Sheehan and George P. Upton painted, a graphic picture of the devastation at City Cemetery:

> *Into these graveyards many fugitives had fled during that Sunday night and Monday morning. ... The occupants were of all classes. Strong men, hard working able bodied men; weak and delicate women; many of the occupants of fashionable dens of vice; refined and cultivated women; merchants, lawyers and bankers; servant men and women, but the great bulk were the families of small tradesmen, and working people of the neighborhood. Of course there were troops of children, all huddled in groups, with backs to the fire, to protect their eyes from the blinding smoke and consuming heat. Incessantly there fell among them the flying sparks and cinders. In vain did these poor fugitives seek to cover their packages of clothing with sand. The fire would fall upon them and set them ablaze. At last the fire approached them; it seized upon the long wooden sidewalks of the streets beyond, and with the speed of lightning traversed block after block, encircling every place with a cordon of fire. The fences one after another caught, the twigs, and scattered lumber, with here and there a house, a stable, or a shed seemed to furnish food enough to carry that fire along. At last it reached the grave yard, the fences caught and blazed;*

the heat prepared everything for the advancing column of fire. Group after group fled before the flame; the straw beds, chairs, tables, the trunks, the bundles of clothes and the household goods, soon were on fire; head board after head board blazed as a brazen mirror reflecting light. The little fences around the burial lots, the scanty trees and shrubbery all took fire, and each fed the rapacious flames. The living had to abandon even the desolate grave yard, and the fire swept from the earth everything that was consumable. Stout trees were burned down below the ordinary level of the soil in which they grew. These cemeteries before the fire were desolate— – one half the dead having been disinterred, and the monuments and valuable adornments removed, and now came the fire to make desolation more desolate, not a vestige remains of anything in these silent cities of the dead save the blackened embers of the once erect grave signs, and of the little property carried there for safety and then overtaken and consumed by the insatiable fire.

...There are no strangers here. There are no ceremonies. The cement of a kindred sorrow has done its work. ...At last the raging sea sweeps by to the northward, following the line of houses, and the most reckless or courageous ... lie down upon the graves to sleep— – the queerest camp that ever gathered under heaven.[11]

In recent years, artist and researcher Pamela Bannos publicly shared the tireless work she had done for years on the history of City Cemetery. Her expansive "Hidden Truths" project has revealed some staggering discrepancies between the long standing records and beliefs, and the reality of the truth. For generations, historians put the numbers of forgotten graves in Lincoln Park at around onea thousand. Bannos discovered that, from the estimated 35,000 burials in City Cemetery (and the adjoining Catholic Cemetery), there were approximately 14,500 disinterments of marked graves, along with about 8,000 bodies from the potter's field, the latter of which were moved to Oak Woods and the Cook County Poor Farm Cemetery (Dunning).

---

11   *Chicago and the Great Conflagration* by Elias Colbert and Everett Chamberlin.

Left behind, then, in Lincoln Park, would be an estimated 13,000 unmarked graves.

Chicago's Gold Coast is the city's most exclusive neighborhood. In these posh mansions just south of North Avenue and the old City Cemetery, ghosts are a dime a dozen, though not many are talked about by their ultra-chic flesh-and-blood housemates.

When, in 1885, Archbishop Patrick Feehan set up housekeeping in a lavish mansion on State Parkway, a large acreage surrounded the dwelling. For this had been the early Catholic cemetery adjoining the "regular" one: City Cemetery. As non-Catholics moved their loved ones to Graceland, Rosehill and Oakwoods, Catholics went to Calvary, on the border between Chicago and Evanston, a town directly north of the city limits.

Well, *some* of them did.

With the corpses (allegedly) gone, the abandoned Archdiocesan expanse was open for suggestions.. Much of the land south of here became Lincoln Park. The rest was sold off for residential development. Yet, while the lakefront and its adjacent neighborhood would become beautiful over the next half century, little did the earliest squatters know that this area was destined to become one of the swankiest neighborhoods in America. Little, too, did they realize that bodies from the empty cemetery would continue to turn up here for the next 100 years.

Fourteen years after the opening of Lincoln Park, Potter Palmer, Chicago's most influential businessman of the day, moved into a million-dollar castle at 1350 N. Lake Shore Drive, fleeing the elite community of Prairie Avenue, south of the city center. In a short time, Palmer's former neighbors followed suit, and the old burial ground began to really glimmer. From then on, Chicago's old and new money would consider the Gold Coast as the ultimate in city living.

Many of the sumptuous residences that arose from this former swamp still stand today, relics of an age of overkill. Living in them are a number of descendants of those first Chicago "haves" and a host of relatively new millionaires as well. Though their origins may vary, many have at least two things in common: they're loaded, and they're haunted.

Since the neighborhood's earliest days, Gold Coasters settling down on Dearborn Parkway, State Parkway, and Astor Street have been aware of a sort of shadow population living with them in these haunts of the rich and famous (a population hailing, presumably, from the old City Cemetery) and the remains that, despite the cemetery's relocation, remained right here, often under the foundations of their houses.

After the first run-ins with partially decomposed corpses during the groundbreaking of the early homes and the hasty disposal of the evidence, residents complained of strange goings-on in their dream homes. As these hauntings arose time and again, would-be builders listened well. Soon, an unspoken understanding prevailed among future homeowners: when remains were unearthed, no expense or effort was spared in properly burying the grisly find.

Even today, this silent pact holds true. When, just recently, at the end of the twentieth century, a wealthy businessman began the total renovation of a grand old structure on State Parkway, he was hardly surprised at the discovery of an early team of contractors and well prepared with an old neighborhood solution.

My cousin, later head of the Sheet Metal Workers Union, was on the job and told me about what went down when the renovation of the elegant brownstone began:

> *The basement floor had to be opened up for plumbing, electrical, and ventilation work.*
>
> *The job had to be dug by hand, by pick and shovel, and the men digging the trenches unearthed human remains. The general contractor on the job had a Native-American laborer, a very spiritual man. When the men working on the trench would disturb any remains, they were told to go upstairs and get this laborer, who would then come down and remove the remains to the side of the trench and say prayers over them.*

Ghost hunters have long known of the haunting of these old cemetery grounds by the dead left behind after the Great Fire, but while several investigations have been done on the public grounds of Lincoln Park and in some of the private homes and businesses of the surrounding area, no investigation had ever been done of the Lincoln Park Zoo, which spread from it original enclosure over a large acreage, including much of the former cemetery grounds.

When, then, the events manager called me in the spring of 2013 about creating a "ghost tour" of the Zoo for patrons as part of its public programming, I was beyond thrilled at the prospect, and we immediately set a date for an initial investigation night.

I knew exactly where I wanted to go on that first visit, because over many years I had been approached via letter, phone call and email about close encounters in, of all places, the women's restroom in the Lion House basement. Time after time, women would report having used the facility and, while washing their hands or applying makeup, seeing in the mirrors men and women dressed in Victorian clothing. On the night of the first investigation that summer, myself and another investigator entered the restroom and were immediately struck by the layout of the room. Rows of sinks lined the two walls, parallel to each other. Above the sinks were rows of mirrors, creating an "infinity" effect from the two walls of mirrors facing each other.

Now, most paranormal investigators will concur that mirrors are one of those things--like salt or water--that have some definite power in the world of the preternatural. Steeped in folklore, these items really do seem to have some importance in the realm of paranormal experience. One theory is that entities can be easily "trapped" in mirrors. Presumably, the spirits enter them to explore the objects they see reflected, but suddenly find themselves engulfed in blackness, on the other side of the mirror's glass--essentially inside the mirror.

This works the opposite way as well. My friend Colleen Nadas, a medium, likes to build and use a tool called "The Devil's Toybox," which is a kind of "ghost trap" comprised of a cube made of inward facing square mirrors, securely taped together at the seams. Investigators use contact microphones to record sounds from inside the box, believing that if a spirit attempts to investigate, it will find itself trapped because of the mirrors and start to make a fuss. Sometimes this "fussing" leads to great electronic voice phenomena, or EVP: recordings of the voices of the angry or frightened ghosts or knocking sounds from inside the box. In the Zoo's Lion House, we instantly theorized that entities were routinely finding themselves stuck in these mirrors due to the effect created by the rows of mirrors facing each other.

Anecdotes collected from the Zoo staff confirmed that staff members had also experienced encounters here, especially hearing a man's voice commanding, "Get out!" Amazingly, when I set up my laptop and began to record for EVP, within a minute I picked up a stern male voice warning, "Get out! There's a woman here!" A future visit by a medium confirmed that one of the male spirits had taken on the task of keeping men--dead and alive--out of the women's restroom.

As we continued our investigation, I took several series of photographs down the row of stalls leading to the end of the facility. During investigations, I like to take fifty to one hundred photos or more of each location to see if any of the frames contain an anomaly. When I played back the recording done during this time, I found that one of the male entities was a bit angry that I wasn't paying as much attention to him as the area I was photographing, because he clearly says, "Will you look at me!"

As is typical with most investigators, I asked if there was anything I could do for the entities who remained in this spot. The same voice, now with a tinge of sadness, answered, "Help me...with leaving." When I asked if there was anything the spirits wanted to tell us about their time on Earth, one can make out the sound of a lion's roar and of the same voice saying, "I miss it."

On a subsequent visit to the Lion House bathroom, I was amazed to find that I had photographed a shadowy figure silhouetted against one of the bathroom stalls. This photograph was one of a sequence of sixty I had snapped, one after another in quick sequence. Only this photo showed the image. The other investigators with me attempted to recreate the shadow by standing against the opposite wall, out of view, but could not.

On the first investigation night, after several hours of research and experiment, we decided to call it a night and began to disable and back up our equipment. I would say that, generally, when an investigator ends an investigation and says "Goodbye!" before turning off a recording device, the entities tend to scramble to say more, especially to give more pleas for help. Not so in the case of this location. At least one of the entities was eager to see us go. In response to my invitation, "Is there anything else you'd like to say before we go?" the sound of--perhaps anxious--footfalls can be heard, along with the words, "Turn out the light. Good night!"

My first exposure to primates as a child was at the old "Children's Zoo" at Chicago's Lincoln Park Zoo: a building next to the Sea Lion pool which focused on education for young children, where my dad would take me as part of our regular "rounds" about the city.

At the Children's Zoo we could watch baby chimps being bottle fed, learn about the varying plumage of birds, and even hold a snake or two. My dad, always the troublemaker, would horrify me by taking off his stocking hat and holding it through the bars of one of the walk-in cages where an active little white headed capuchin was housed. Invariably, the little guy would grab Dad's hat, and a keeper would eventually have to go in and coax the little guy to give it back.

Little did I know while I watched that tiny creature pulling on my dad's cap that Lincoln Park Zoo was one of the most important centers for primate research in the world. Named for a former Zoo director and world-renowned ape researcher, today the Lester E. Fisher Center for the Study and Conservation of Apes brings together researchers and organizations from around the world.

Dr. Lester Fisher is a familiar name to native Chicagoans born between 1960 and 1975, as the good doctor was a popular fixture on WGN's beloved Ray Rayner Show: a morning news show for kids which featured news, weather and sports, comedy and musical sketches, arts and crafts and more. Animals were an important part of the show. Children looked forward to the weekly visits from Chelveston, a white duck who lived at the Animal Kingdom pet shop on Milwaukee Avenue, as Rayner fed the duck and chased him around the studio, trying to get him to jump into a basin of water, which usually ended up with Rayner being much wetter than Chelveston.

Rayner also took occasional "field trips" to Lincoln Park Zoo, in a wonderful segment called The Ark in the Park. During the segments the host would visit with Dr. Fisher, who would introduce viewers to one of the thousands of breeds housed at the Zoo and talk about their habitats.

Lincoln Park Zoo's Regenstein Center houses the finest collection of endangered apes in the world. Before it was built, the Zoo's apes were housed in the modern Great Ape House (completed in 1976), which today is office and meeting space, topped by an enchanting carousel featuring endangered species rather than horses. Previous to the erection of that facility, the great apes made the old primate house their home, which is today called the Helen Brach Primate House. This structure was one of the original Zoo buildings but was remodeled in the 1990s to remove the cells and bars and recreate, instead, a two-story faux "jungle" of trees and water, fronted by thick glass and enhanced by an outdoor habitat for the warmer months. The Primate House today is home to monkeys, lemurs, gibbons and tamarins who mesmerize guests for hours with their antics. Perhaps the ghost of my dad's little capuchin is still there, waiting for the tall guy with the hat to come back.

Until the opening of the Great Ape House in 1976, Lester Fisher's office was housed in the Primate House as well. You can still see the door to it, on the left as you enter the beautiful arched entryway to the historic structure. Though he was a famous and much-loved fixture at the Zoo, Dr. Fisher's popularity was eclipsed by another familiar of the Primate House: the world-renowned great ape known as Bushman, one of the most famous animals ever held in captivity. Often featured in newsreels, Bushman had been the pet of a Cameroon minister's daughter before being sold to the Zoo in 1930 for $3,500, or about $50,000 today.

The cuddly creature she'd called "my sweet little boy" as a child grew into a 550 pound hulk who drew millions of visitors during his tenure at Lincoln Park Zoo. His massive girth was a shuddering thing to behold. As one reporter observed, Bushman appeared *like a nightmare that escaped from darkness into daylight who has exchanged its insubstantial form for 550 pounds of solid flesh. His face is one that might be expected to gloat through the troubled dreams that follow overindulgence. His hand is the kind of thing a sleeper sees reaching for him just before he wakes up screaming.*

But Bushman's real appeal lay not in his ability to terrify, but to charm. Visitors stood for hours watching his antics, which included throwing food and dung at patrons with razor sharp precision. In the fall of 1950 Bushman escaped from his cage, meandering through the primate house for hours until a garter snake scared the giant back to his enclosure.

Earlier that year, an illness which threatened death had caused more than 100,000 visitors to pay their last respects. Bushman survived-- briefly--and passed away the next winter, on New Year's Day 1951. His empty cage became a point of pilgrimage for weeks after his death. His enormous frame was preserved by taxidermy and put on permanent display at Chicago's Field Museum of Natural History. In 2013, Winifred Hope, the girl who had loved Bushman like a baby brother during his earliest days in West Africa, visited the specimen in the spring of 2013 at the age of 92.

The emotional and important history of the Primate House made it a definite "to do" on our list of locations to investigate at Lincoln Park Zoo. I especially wanted to see if we could pick up any residual voices in Dr. Fisher's erstwhile office.

Dr. Fisher, of this writing, is very much alive; however, often we find that when someone is passionately tied to a location for many years, their voice, their smell, and even their physical form can leave a lasting impression which can sometimes be picked up by future generations. With his intense connection to the Zoo and to primate research here, would we find that Dr. Fisher, upon retirement, had left part of himself behind?

That first night we set up a laptop computer to record for EVP in Fisher's old office space. We left the laptop inside, closing the door and going on to investigate elsewhere. Since we were not trying to communicate with an intelligent entity but simply pick up residual sounds, there was no need for us to remain and ask questions, which is the usual method of collecting EVP from discarnate entities.

Disappointingly we did not pick up any voices from Fisher's office, but we did find that the laptop had mysteriously ended the recording and started two successive ones--a truly impossible feat with no one in the locked room to stop and start the recording button.

While the recording was going on, we went on to the larger Primate House to investigate. With us was Colleen Nadas, a medium who picked up numerous entities in the building, most of them the energies of children. Fascinatingly, several years later Dave Olson and his group, Chicago Paranormal Investigators, recorded what sounded like a little girl saying, "I want to go to the Lincoln Zoo." During the same investigation, Olson's group was able to record, with a thermal camera, anomalous moving forms along the floor of the corridor.

That same night, I had been recording near the interior part of the entrance and went out into the vestibule to listen to the recording, hoping I'd picked something up. After a few minutes I shut off my laptop because I heard, coming from inside the building, a high pitched screaming which sounded like one of the lemurs shrieking at the top of its lungs. I had several teams with me that night as my guests and thought one of the members was agitating the animals. After several minutes of this relentless screaming, I went to tell the culprit to stop annoying the creature so we wouldn't be asked to leave. As soon as I opened the interior door, the shrieking stopped. To my amazement, I found upon inquiring of the various investigators that not one person had heard the hair curling sounds or picked them up on their recording devices.

Later that evening, I sat on the floor against the wall, recording with my laptop and softly asking questions of any entities which might be present. Asking, "How many are here?" I received the answer, "Many. Like meeeeeee....." And, "We're all here." I then asked, "Are you an animal or a keeper?" In response, a male voice with an Australian accent responded, "Who cares?" When I asked if there were any animals or humans from another country, a voice responded, "I've been so many places." This particular clip is an example of an entity using an investigator's voice to create words, as this voice sounds like mine, but of course with the unnatural rhythm so common to EVP. Very interestingly, another voice mentioned Julie, the events manager who was with us that night. We had all been very, very busy that spring but Julie was eager to set up another investigation so that we could add more material to the Zoo ghost tour that fall. Thanks to her efforts, we finally got everyone together on schedule to come out for an investigation. The entities in the Primate House evidently knew it had been hard to coordinate, because when I asked, "Are you glad we are here?" A voice says, "I love it. Julie caught you."

Of course, in all of the locations investigated, there was the possibility that entities were attached to the bodies who had been interred at the City Cemetery which formerly stood here. During one investigation, Dave Olson and the Chicago Paranormal Investigators asked, "Are you part of the cemetery that was here?" A male voice answered, "Yes, I was."

THE HANCOCK CENTER

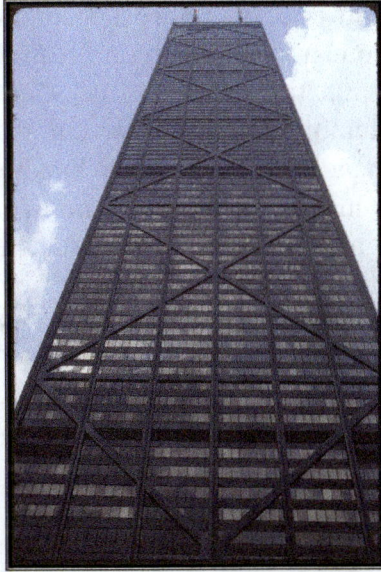

12

In urban areas around the world, architecture's brilliant progress has been checked by many faults. For every successful design, there are ten that fail—aesthetically, financially, or environmentally. Most troublesome have been the so-called "sick buildings" that have caused everything from nausea and headaches to brain tumors and cancer, due to difficulties with exhaust and ventilation systems, mold growth, and other quirks. In Chicago, one of the most controversial buildings in this birthplace of skyscrapers is believed by Chicago paranormal experts to have a much more malicious quality. Since its completion in 1968, the John Hancock Center has been the site of multiple murders, suicides, and deadly "accidents." Why? Windy City occultists are convinced that it is the very design of the place that causes its residents and workers to often take a turn for the worse.

The John Hancock Center was designed as a trapezoidal structure by its chief architect, Bruce Graham, under the counsel of Fazlur Khan, a structural engineer at the esteemed Chicago firm of Skidmore, Owings

12   The Hancock Tower is sometimes called "Satan's Skyscraper." (Author's photo)

& Merrill. Khan proposed the shape as an economical way to combine larger office spaces on the lower floors with smaller apartment units on the upper levels. It wasn't long before some Chicagoans began to question the "innocent" trapezoidal design as a poor one. Was the building's form, in fact, the shape of things to come?

A little over three years after the Hancock's completion, a twenty-nine-year-old Chicago woman named Lorraine Kowalski fell to her death from her boyfriend's ninetieth-floor Hancock Center apartment. To this day, detectives are dumbfounded by the event; the building's windows are capable of withstanding more than two hundred pounds of pressure per square foot and winds of more than 150 miles per hour, yet Kowalski actually broke through the glass. Four years later, a transmitter technician for a local radio station plunged to his death from the ninety-seventh-floor offices of his television station. Just three months later, a twenty-seven-year-old tenant "fell" from his ninety-first-floor apartment while studying for an exam at breakfast. In 1978, a thirty-one-year-old woman shot a man to death in his home on the Hancock's sixty-fifth floor, and in 1998, beloved comedian Chris Farley was found dead in the entrance hall of his sixtieth-floor apartment. Most recently, in March of 2002, a twenty-five-foot aluminum scaffold fell from the building's forty-third floor, crushing three cars, killing three women, and injuring eight others. All of these incidents were called by detectives and journalists baffling, inexplicable and seemingly unmotivated.

Many years before construction on the Hancock began, the area it would occupy was part of one of the most luxurious residential districts in the city. This neighborhood, still known as Streeterville, was already thought to be a cursed tract of land. Cap Streeter, its namesake, was a ragtag former sea captain who made a living ferrying passenger between Chicago and Milwaukee on a beat-up old schooner he owned with his wife. After the vessel literally washed up on the Chicago shore during a storm, Cap decided to settle down in the city for good. He staked claim to the very parcel of land on which he had run ashore: prime lakefront property much in demand by Chicago's first families. Cap found the land so lovely that he decided to share the beauty. He set up shop in the old Tremont Hotel, selling tracts of "his" land to willing buyers. Soon a legion of squatters peppered the lakefront, angering Chicago's elite and the city council that served them. When the city repeatedly tried to run off the trespassers, Cap and company responded with shotguns, batons and all manner of homemade weapons.

The battle over "Cap's" land—which he called Streeterville—raged until the man's dying hour... and beyond. On his deathbed, Cap cursed "his" land and swore that no one would ever be happy on it again. Then is the "Curse of Cap Streeter" the source of the Hancock's problem?

Perhaps. Or perhaps not.

It seems that, by now, everyone knows the legends of this mysterious structure. Along with the numerous apparently unexplained deaths by suicide, homicide and freak accident, rumor has it that a colony of spiders lives on the outside of the building and makes its way, mysteriously, up one side and down the other once a year.

In fact, the Hancock isn't the only building to suffer a seasonal spider plague. Numerous Chicago skyscrapers attract the so-called "high rise spiders" (more properly called *Lariniodes Sclopetarius*). It's the strong updrafts outside these lakeside structures that allow the wingless creatures to ascend as high as five thousand feet along the outer walls, in search of insects. Arachnophobes would do well to avoid dining at the Signature Room at the Hancock—it's posh, 95th-floor restaurant—in the springtime, when the breathtaking vistas may include some of these beasts staring back at you.

The spiders don't really like human flesh, but they will resort to it if their preferred prey is scarce, such as if they find their way inside your hotel room. Each spring, you'll find high-rise hotels along the lakefront warning guests to keep their windows closed.

Another legend of the Hancock is that the building inspired the "Ghostbusters" film script. According to the legend—which was told to me by a tour guest but which I've as yet been unable to verify—Dan Ackroyd visited his friend, John Belushi, when the latter was living in one of the Hancock apartments. Ackroyd and Harold Ramis knew they wanted to make a movie about a ragtag group of ghost hunters living in New York, but they were reportedly having trouble coming up with a storyline. That weekend, they say, Belushi regaled his friend with harrowing tales of the strange deaths that had occurred at the Hancock.

Then Belushi told Ackroyd another strange story about the building—
one that has lived in infamy in local legend: That the late Church of Satan
founder Anton LaVey was born on the property where this enigmatic
structure now stands and, moreover, that LaVey himself had warned the
City of Chicago against building the Hancock Center at all.

LaVey, the colorful character who professed a "religion" of individualism
and materialism --and who wrote a whole bunch of (frankly pretty
interesting) essays during his reign as the self-proclaimed high priest
of his own church--was born in Chicago on April 11, 1930 and died
in San Francisco, after a larger-than-life adulthood in his iconic black-
painted house. In his sometimes critically-acclaimed volume of essays,
The Devil's Notebook, LaVey put forth his now-infamous "Law of
the Trapezoid," in which he referenced the very building in question,
believing that the strange angles of the Hancock and other modern
structures could wreak havoc on the tenants inside:

> *The most disturbing shape of all is a trapezoid in its myriad*
> *forms. A perfect trapezoid is a frustrated pyramid . . . . A*
> *trapezoid says to your unconscious, 'I am here, solid as can*
> *be, more massive than an ordinary block, but something's*
> *missing and it bothers you.' Of course, you know what's*
> *missing: a triangular top, like the one with an eye on the*
> *back of a dollar bill. Don't let that little pyramid with the*
> *bright eye fool you. That's to draw your attention away from*
> *the real thing: the big trapezoid beneath it. All competent*
> *magicians are masters of misdirection, and the Masons who*
> *designed the seal knew a thing or two.*

> *. . . The John Hancock Center in Chicago looms like a*
> *sentinel in its black splendor, its sloping sides and dark color*
> *presenting a brooding spectacle with its twin devil horns/*
> *antennae bisecting its top and continuing the frustum up and*
> *away into the sky. That its history is already grim is, to me,*
> *quite understandable.*

LaVey's "Law" had its roots, as any Lovecraftian scholar will instantly
recognize, in the stories and ideas of H.P. Lovecraft and his tendency to
link the paranormal with architecture that is somehow "off."

But what of LaVey's sensational claim that he, in fact, was born on the very property where the building would be erected some forty years after his birth? The truth is that LaVey--born Howard Stanton Levey--does have a rather mysterious birth record, but only because his parents do not seem to have had a common residence at the time of Howard's arrival. Michael Joseph Levey, Anton (Howard)'s father was born in Chicago in November of 1903, and married Gertrude Augusta Coultron, daughter of Russian and Ukrainian emigrants to Ohio. Michael was a salesman who changed jobs often, dabbling in numerous products with myriad companies. Though no marriage record could be located for he and Gertrude, 1930 found the then-27-year-olds pregnant with their first child.

Fascinating connections have been made online to a Michael and Gertrude Levy, who in 1930 lived near the Evanston, Illinois border of Chicago, in the historically and architecturally pristine Casa Bonita apartments. But though the connection would be lovely--the building is known by many paranormal researchers to have a "dark" feel and history--the connection is nonexistent. Anton's mother, Gertrude, is listed as residing with her parents in Garfield Park just five days after Anton's birth.

At the time of Anton's birth, his mother, Gertrude Levey, was living in her family apartment at 3820 West Maypole Avenue, in the (then) rather affluent Garfield Park neighborhood. But while both the U.S. Census of 1930 lists "Gertrude Levey" as both "daughter" and "boarder" on the Census chart recorded April 16, 1930--five days after Anton's birth--neither Anton (Howard) Levey nor his father, Michael, are recorded as members of the household. In fact, in 1930, the only M. Levey residing in Chicago with a telephone registered to his name was an "M.L. Levey" living in the 500 block of West Monroe Street. As for rumors that the young Anton may have been born in a relative's home at the Hancock site--a common occurrence well into the 1940s--a look at the infant's birth certificate, right, nixes that possibility. The document clearly states that Howard Stanton Levey was born on April 11, 1930 at the Franklin Boulevard Community Hospital (later Sacred Heart Hospital). The certificate also states that both of his parents resided at the Maypole Avenue address.

By 1933, the Leveys had left Chicago, presumably on the heels of a new sales job in Modesto, California, where they moved into a ten year-old bungalow at 416 Sycamore Avenue. The entire family would remain in the St. Francisco Bay area for the rest of their lives, but little Howard would never cease to feel his Chicago roots--even going so far as to "plant" some from his own imagination.

One last legend of the Hancock deserves a mention. They say that the building was actually responsible for the death of little Heather O'Rourke, the captivating blonde girl who starred in the *Poltergeist* films. In fact, *Poltergeist 3* filmed partly in the Hancock Center, and legend has it that O'Rourke, who suffered from Chron's Disease, had enjoyed some better health but fell sick again during the filming of the third installation of the franchise, dying during post production.

I was well aware of this, what seemed just one of those "cursed film" rumors out of Hollywood, when I was giving a coach tour one day to a group of seniors from out of town. During the lunch stop, I was eating alone in the bar of the Fireside restaurant on Ravenswood Avenue, a place where we often had a meal break during our tours. The group was lunching in the fireplace room off the bar, and since the restrooms were in the bar, several tour guests stopped and talked with me as they made their way to and from the restrooms. One of these was a very nice gentleman who told me that he was enjoying the tour very much, and that it was all new to him. He had never, he explained, had any interest in the paranormal until his granddaughter passed away. This was not the first time I had spoken to someone who, after such a devastating loss, became interested in ghost stories. But before I could even express my condolences, he shocked me by saying, "My granddaughter was Heather O'Rourke."

He went on to tell me that, while she'd had a lot of health issues during the filming of the last movie—which included scenes in the Hancock— Heather had been doing much better since it wrapped. However, during post-production, she had returned to Chicago to do a promotional event for the film. That had been a radio show recorded in the Hancock Center as well. After that trip, her condition took a last turn for the worst.

She died soon after at Rady Children's Hospital in San Diego.

CURSE OF THE CORN COBS

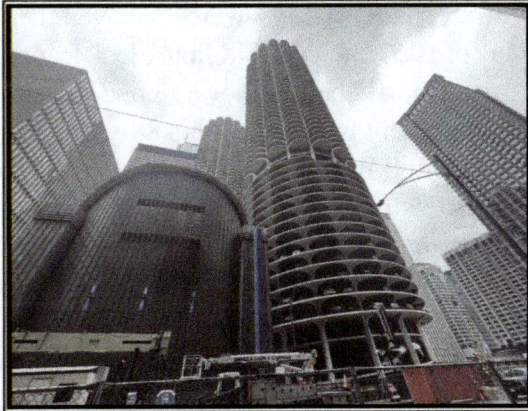

13

The Hancock is hardly alone in its haunting of the city's skyline. While hosting a ghost tour for the Chicago History Museum some years ago now, I was approached by a young woman who works near Marina City, the twin "corncobs" on Chicago's riverfront which have been an unmistakable part of the city since their completion in 1962. Like many who live or work in or near the complex, which includes hundreds of apartments, a rather unnerving parking garage, and the House of Blues music hall, the passenger on my tour wanted to know, "What's up with Marina City?"

By her question, she was referring to the endless stream of reports of apparitions, shadow people, malfunctioning electronics, icy drafts, and feelings of depression or oppression which have plagued residents for decades--but only in the East Tower. Why the prevalence of phenomena . . . and why only in one of the buildings?

A visit to the *Chicago Tribune* Archives offers some chilling possibilities. During construction of the towers, in 1961, three workers were killed when a scaffold plummeted a full 43 stories. That same year, six men were badly injured when a workers' elevator plummeted; a seventh was injured trying to help them. The next year, in 1962, worker William

---

13   Marina City towers (Photo by Mike Huberty)

Jones was stricken by a dizzy spell while working on a scaffold at the 40th floor. He plunged to his death on the State Street Bridge below.

Accidents at the construction site were joined by a long string of dark deaths between 1966 and 1976. In August of 1966, Roy Holland, a real estate developer, was found to have been dead for three weeks when his body--and three suicide notes--were discovered in his 48th floor apartment. In May of 1967, 39-year-old June Fleck leapt from her fiance's 50th floor apartment shortly before they planned to marry. In January of 1969, a retired government worker shot his 88-year old mother and then turned the gun on himself in their 46th floor apartment. In June of 1973, 42- year old Sandra Easton, a computer programmer, leapt to her death from her 52nd floor apartment, crashing through the canvas roof of the complex's ice rink (today the site of Smith & Wollensky restaurant). Just two years earlier, Easton had been saved from an earlier attempt to jump. In 1972, 25-year-old Gloria Kirpatrick, 39th floor resident and manager of the Marina City Theater (now the House of Blues) was stabbed to death outside the building. In January of 1976, 25-year-old Kenneth Parvin fell to his death from a 57th floor apartment, landing between the two towers on Marina City Drive. Whether the death was accidental or intentional, or the result of foul play, was not known.

Many years ago, I was chatting with Rick Kogan, the longtime Chicago journalist and son of historian Herman Kogan, as we waited to be part of a panel at the Printer's Row Book Fair one summer. He shared with me the memory that, during the "swinging sixties" and into the '70s, when Marina City was where many of the young and hip lived, it wasn't uncommon for partygoers in the buildings' apartments to overindulge in drugs and alcohol and attempt a sort of "dare." Spurred on by fellow partiers, some foolish souls would try to make their way around the entire round building by edging their way along the outside of one apartment balcony rail to the next. More than one hapless soul fell to death during these exercises.

Marina City apartments contain almost no interior right angles. The residential floors consist of a circular hallway wrapped around the elevator core, with 16 wedge-shaped apartments arranged around the hallway. Each wedge is trimmed with a semi-circular balcony outside a glass wall. Architect Bertrand Goldberg explained during construction that the design of each tower was meant to provide a widening vista to residents as they entered their apartments.   From the small entrance, at the narrowest part of the wedge, the apartments would open up to the wide glass wall and even wider balcony, offering the city and the lake outside--like living in a "treehouse" was how the architect described it. Could it be that this well-meant design has actually inspired some residents to take the widening vistas one step further? Could the contrast between the tiny apartment and the wide open space outside have caused an impulse for escape in more than one tenant?

Though the jury may always be out on the answer, the established truth remains that the residue of some tragic and troublesome events--and their unfortunate victims—continues to make its home in the mysterious digs at 300 North State Street.

THE TRIBUNE TOWER

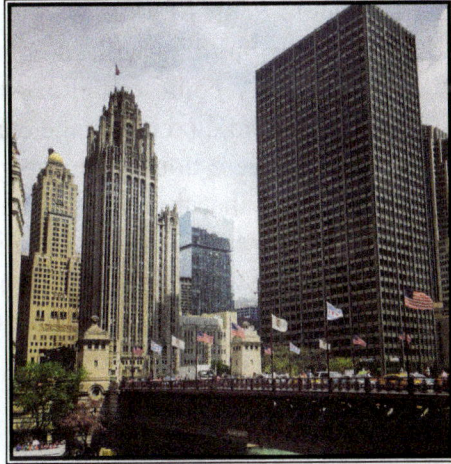

14

One other iconic Chicago structure deserves mention on our tour: the former lair of one of Chicago's most headstrong and influential personalities: Colonel Robert McCormick.

When he first laid eyes on the now iconic Tribune Tower at the Northeast end of the Michigan Avenue bridge, the high priest of Chicago architecture, Louis Sullivan, called the flying buttresses and heavy piers at the pinnacle "the monster on top."

The harshness might have been inflated by emotion. Not only were the architects—John Mead Howell s and Raymond Hood--from New York; the latter had been working as a radiator cover designer when the pair won the Tribune commission.

The "monster" is not the only curious detail in the building. Numerous "grotesques" cover the building. These are not gargoyles but rather characters representing facets of the journalistic life: a camera-toting owl, an ape, an elephant holding its nose. Characters from Aesop's fables join them in a screen over the main entrance--those creatures

---

hailing from the age-old tales of virtue and vice. If you look closely, you'll even find among them the *Tribune*'s editors, Joseph Patterson and Colonel Robert McCormick. Even the architects make an appearance here; Howells and Hood peek out from the top of the screen.

Before the *Tribune*--and its sister radio station, WGN--left the building, my dear friend and colleague Scott Markus was invited to conduct a paranormal investigation of the building with radio host Patti Vasquez. She and her crew had apparently come to believe that the late, great Bob Collins--a WGN reporter who died in a plane crash in 2000--might be haunting the studios which were housed on the ground floor of the Tribune Tower. I knew firsthand that there was something a little "off" about that space, because for years I made the middle of the night trip down to Tribune Tower to swap ghost stories on the air with the wonderful broadcaster Dave Plier. Literally every year we did the show we would have lights flash on and off during the show, doors lock themselves or microphones pop on and off.

And so Scott started the investigation in the WGN studios, but only a faint knocking was heard by the team during their time there. Undaunted, Vazquez led the team up to a boardroom a few floors above. This turned out to be THE boardroom--the place where reporters were made and destroyed, stories were planned, buried and resurrected. As Markus monitored the rooom with various investigation tools, things began to hum. A deep drop in temperature--a "cold spot"--registered for an instant before the thermal scanner rose to normal again. EMF meters spiked for a second then rested. Most telling of all--no pun intended-- was a very distinct, audible whisper that everyone heard.

During the course of the evening, Markus got a chance to talk to security guards in the tower. As he points out (and I concur one hundred percent) these guys are the very best source of information about potential hauntings and other paranormal activity. When the team asked the guards if any part of the building seemed haunted, they did not hesitate.

"The 24th floor."

When pressed for a reason, the guards shared that someone had committed suicide by jumping from that floor--and that the energy from that is actually palpable in that area where this unfortunate person spent his last moments. Markus and the crew knew this was no invented tale; the guards wouldn't even enter the floor after unlocking the door for the investigation team. Later, Markus would discover in his research that a suicide had occurred in 2011, though no mention was made of a floor number.

Much more likely is that a very different—but also deeply troubled— spirit is driving away even the security guards on floor 24: the Colonel himself. For this was his lair, the home of his office, the throne room of the king. Outfitted with gleaming marble and dark, handsome paneling, it was where McCormick ran his empire. And as Blair Kamin, a longtime Tribune reporter, was quick to point out, it wasn't included in the building's landmark protection, which only protects the exterior and the main lobby.

In paranormal investigation and ghostlore, one of the motivations we surmise for why souls remain here on earth is *control*. Sometimes, it seems, someone who built something so big, so great, so impressive . . . well, they just don't seem to want to let it go, to let it fall into the hands of someone almost certainly less dedicated, less invested, less involved. The Colonel was nothing if not the poster child for involvement. He owned the *paper mill* that provided the *Tribune*'s newsprint, for crying out loud. I would venture a guess that, even now, he doesn't want to relinquish his place at the head of his empire. Or perhaps the right phrase is "especially now"-- when that empire has been sold by the pound and his reporters and editors given the boot.

Scott and I talked about the investigation after it was complete. He and I both wonder if at least some of the activity in the building--and maybe even some of the less-than-rosy life of the Colonel--stems from the extensive collection of mostly ill-gotten "souvenirs" literally embedded in the building.

In fact, almost 150 pieces from structures and locations from every part of the world have made their way into the walls of the Tribune Tower, a tradition started by McCormick himself when, in the midst of fighting in World War I Belgium, he pocketed a fragment of the ruins of Apres Cathedral. The Colonel directed his foreign correspondents to add to the collection. And so they did.

Today you'll find a staggering cache of treasures sunk in the tower's limestone: a piece of the Forbidden City dating to 1421; a stone from the Alamo; a piece of moon rock from the Apollo 15 mission; a portion of the Chicago Union Stockyards; a rock from the "treasure cave" of Mark Twain's "Injun Joe" in Hannibal, Missouri; a piece of marble from the same quarry mined to build the Parthenon; a chunk of Lincoln's tomb in Springfield, Illinois; a portion of Admiral Byrd's base in Antarctica; part of John Brown's cabin; a chunk of prison wall from Andersonville--the Civil War's most notorious--; a shard from the Berlin Wall; a beam from the ruins of the World Trade Center.

Now, if there's one thing paranormal investigators know--from hearing stories or learning the hard way--it's to take only memories from sites of tragedy, turmoil or disaster. I could tell tales all day of investigators who, for example, decided to pocket a rock from the legendary Bell Witch Cave in Tennessee, a paint chip from the haunted Sallie House in Kansas, or a handful of soil from notorious Bachelors Grove. Then I'm sure Markus could tell them all day tomorrow.

Some years back now, I bought one of the bricks from the St. Valentine's Day Massacre wall where Moran's men were lined up and shot that frigid morning so long ago—a story we'll visit later in this book. "The Chicago Bricks," they call them. The bricks, as I've told you, are supposed to be cursed. I used to tell people about my possession of one of them, "Nothing bad has happened to me!" Then I started to think about that a little more, and I started to wonder about some directions my life had taken since I bought that brick.

A few years ago, at his request, I lent the brick to a friend who wanted to conduct paranormal experiments on it. He asked me when I needed it back.

I told him, "No rush."

Every once in a while, I say a little prayer for him.

THE FIELD MUSEUM

15

Originally founded as the Columbian Museum of Chicago, the city's Field Museum of Natural History was born in conjunction with the World's Fair of 1893, the Columbian Exposition, where the city displayed massive collections, researchers had gathered into anthropological and biological displays.

After the Fair, the collection was moved into the old Palace of Fine Arts—the only Fair building which remains on the old Fairgrounds. In the early 1920s, the museum moved its collections from its exposition site in Jackson Park to its current home on the lakefront, where it fixes one point in the triangle of institutions comprising Chicago's popular "museum campus": the Field, the Adler Planetarium, and the Shedd Aquarium, all connected by landscaped pedestrian pathways. With more than 20 million specimens crammed into its many halls and storerooms, the Field has retained, many times magnified, its original power to thrill the audiences that stream through the museum's exhibits season upon season.

Part of the mystique of the Field can be explained by the cultural diversity of its collections, artifacts dripping with ancient intrigue and reeking of esoterica. Another part can be traced to the army of staff members that

15   The specimens of Lions of Tsavo at the Field Museum today. Via Creative Commons under-Share Alike 3.0 Unported, 2.5 Generic, 2.0 Generic and 1.0 Generic license.

toil behind the scenes and around the clock in its countless labs and workrooms. Here, biologists, anthropologists, geologists, and zoologists carry out their research, registering anywhere from uneventful to earth-shattering.

This double-edged intrigue has led to the telling of many tales about Chicago's Field Museum. When, in 1996, the film The Ghost and the Darkness was released, chronicling the history of the so-called "Man-eaters of Tsavo," a pair of African lions who killed more than 130 railroad workers in the late nineteenth century, longtime rumors re-surfaced regarding the lions' carcasses, which have been part of the Field's collections since the mid-1920s, when they were sold to the museum by Lieutenant Colonel John Henry Patterson, who shot the lions in 1898. Patterson, chief engineer of the British government's project to build a railway bridge over East Africa's Tsavo River, wrung his hands for nine long months as scores of his men reportedly fell prey to the lions, who were guessed to have resorted to man-eating out of sheer hunger when an outbreak of disease killed off much of their natural prey.

The Lions of Tsavo, now highlighted with a detailed exhibit at the Field, are worthy of the story attributed to their name. Though their taxidermied appearance comes up shy of the lions' original statures (one measured more than nine and a half feet at the time of death), their dreadful natures still seem nearly tangible. It is not surprising that the legend of the animals, enhanced by the mystique of their African origin and dramatically underscored by their imposing physical presence, has given rise to new stories of strange behavior: peripheral glimpses of movement in the lions' display case, shifting of the animals' positions between viewings, their occasional disappearance altogether, and terrifying growls emanating from the exhibit hall.

One archivist at the Field told me in the spring of 1996 that she had seen one of the lions walking through the museum halls while working alone one night. Security guards reportedly called Chicago Police, thinking that a bobcat had somehow gotten into the museum—or perhaps an escapee from the Lincoln Park Zoo. No trace of any live animal was found.

The Field is also home to a piece of a "cursed" meteorite, the Elbogen meteorite that fell to Earth in the 15th century in Loket in the Kingdom of Bohemia, present day Czech Republic. Legend held that the meteorite was in fact a much-maligned count of Loket Castle, located in the current Czech Republic, who had turned to stone after being cursed by a witch and struck by lightning. Citizens and rulers alike maintained such a fear of the object that it was chained up in the dungeon of the castle for generations.

Another of the museum's permanent exhibits, Inside Ancient Egypt, has also played host to a number of paranormal reports, namely of the sound of screams coming from the rooms housing the mummy displays that, some claim, inspired the film *The Relic*, an ancient-horror movie set in Chicago's natural history museum. One mummy in particular, an ancient fellow named Harwa, was reported to occasionally catapult his own sarcophagus off the display stand and onto the floor, several feet away, after coming to live at the museum. Security guards were said to discover the movement after investigating a loud, gunshot-like sound that preceded the phenomenon. Though many believe that Harwa took midnight strolls through the museum on the nights when his casket went haywire, few have seen the man behind the mummy in action.

Yet, some staff members admit to odd activity around the ancient Egyptian, and employees like Pamela Buczkowske, a circulation clerk at the museum, have their own twilight run-ins with a decidedly Egyptian manifestation in the building's darkening hallways:

> *I had been at the Field Museum for about two years. One evening after closing I was headed back to my office. I had taken the east center staircase down to the ground level. Off to my left was a short hallway I used to get back to where I worked. The hall is all but gone now. A new elevator was installed there, and the Egypt store was housed in that area*

> *As I walked down the stairs, I was surprised to see what I thought was a visitor coming toward me. Normal closing time was five o'clock; we had been closed for twenty minutes already. What didn't dawn on me until later was the fact that I could not see the upper body of the person. A shadow covered it at any angle.*

> *I hurried up to the person to tell them that the museum was closed and he or she (I couldn't tell if it was a man or woman)*

would have to leave. But suddenly, the figure turned into the Egypt exhibit. I was practically on the person's heels, yet when I entered the exhibit, there was no one there. There wasn't even the sound of footfalls. I walked around the dark exhibit for a few minutes and found nothing.

Now, there are three ways to get out of the exhibit, and one gets locked at 4:45, on the first floor. The other two are on the ground floor, and I checked them out. One was locked, and the other would have brought the person right to me.

At first, I didn't really think I saw a ghost, and I wasn't scared. I did a little bit of investigating and found out a few things that I didn't realize at that time. One was the lighting. It wasn't dark enough to cover any part of the person I saw. Two was that the person never even acknowledged my presence. He or she had to have seen me coming toward them. The third thing occurred to me when a guard and I re-enacted what I saw. The lighting was the same and, as I'd suspected, there was no shadow over the upper part of his body.

I could see him perfectly.

THE DEVIL BABY OF HULL HOUSE

16

As a champion of women's independence and the founder of one of progressivism's most controversial institutions, much was asked of Jane Addams, one of the first social workers and among the most influential of the nation's progressivist leaders. Addams was able to provide most of what she was asked for: shelter to the homeless, food to the hungry, encouragement to the hopeless, protection from abusive injustice. But there came a brief period in the life of her pioneering settlement house, Hull House, when the needs of its visitors became insatiable-when women began arriving there by the handful demanding to see "The Devil Baby."

Stories of "devil children" or "devil kids" were not new. Other such tales had peppered the headlines in the late 19th and early 20th centuries. In 1888, a Polish neighborhood just south of Cleveland, Ohio, was searching for the father of a devil child, "red in color, covered with hair, having incipient horns and tail, and claw-like hands, and wing-like protuberances on the back." Several years later, A Minnesota woman went mad after giving birth to a "devil child" after turning away a Bible salesman who knocked on her door. The woman is said to have proclaimed she'd rather have the devil in her house than such a book,

16   At the height of its operation, Hull House was surrounded by twelve other buildings, hosting every kind of social service imaginable. (Public Domain)

after which the salesman apparently put some sort of hex on her, cursing the imminent birth. Years later, Detroit was rocked by the news of a similar "devil kid" who refused to eat food, instead snatching coals from the stove to munch on with its full set of sharp teeth, between bouts of blaspheming and mockery of its poor parents.

In all of these instances and others, stories of these diabolical children were sensations, leading to alleged offers of carnival and museum operators to "buy" the children, hawkers charging money to see them, and bewildered parents fending off throngs of visitors certain that they harbored the children. For each of the stories, there was an attendant backstory: the woman who turned away the salesman, or—in another—a woman who scoffed at a religious icon. In still another case, a woman had done no more than seen a play featuring a demonic character.

The Hull House baby was different. There was no doubt on the streets of Chicago that the baby had been born in a tenement on the Near West Side and brought to Hull House by its beleaguered parents. But unlike the other stories, the backstory of this child differed, depending on who was telling it. There were different cultural specifics, but a moral common to them all: the father of the baby had been punished with the evil offspring for his ingratitude for the expected baby or mistreatment of his pregnant wife and her cultural traditions.

Italian women described a young Catholic girl who had foolishly married an atheist. After she hung a portrait of the Blessed Virgin on their apartment wall, her husband ripped it down, proclaiming that he'd rather have the Devil in the house than such a picture. The Devil Baby was his punishment for that preference.

A Jewish version described the sheepish mother of a handful of daughters and a heartless husband in search of a son. When his wife became pregnant again, the husband clearly announced his preference that she give birth to the Devil before another girl. That bitter proclamation sealed the child's fate.

Just as the causes of the catastrophe varied, so did descriptions of the resulting imp. Though most described a simple homed baby, the more animated narrators added a tail or hooves. Many told of how the child had been born blaspheming and cursing its parents with unimaginable language. In other accounts, the child was fond of smoking cigars and laughing incessantly at its poor parents. Finally, after struggling to control the damned thing, the father hopelessly took it to the heroine of Hull House, Jane Addams herself. Allegedly, Hull House workers had the baby taken to a local church for baptism, but it struggled out of the priest's grasp and began to dance along the back pews. Unable to pacify the evil infant, Addams kept it locked under supervision in an upstairs room at Hull House, where, according to most later versions of the story, it eventually died.

After the first group of women pushed through the front door demanding a look at the child, the parade of the curious appeared unstoppable. Each day for six weeks, women of every class and culture streamed into the settlement house hoping to return home with a tale of the alleged incarnation. Each day, Addams turned them away with growing annoyance at what she saw as a pathetic oppression of immigrant women by their Old World superstitions, and "the 'contagion of emotion' added to that 'aesthetic sociability' which impels any one of us to drag the entire household to the window when a procession comes into the street or a rainbow appears in the sky."

Bewildered by the story's hold on the public imagination, yet unable to persuade the curious of the tale's falsehood, Addams resorted to private interviews with each of the older visitors. In the course of these sessions, she discovered a common quality of desperation among them. Listening with interest to their versions of the stories and the circumstances of their own lives, Addams became aware that the tale was serving a serious need-that of exhausted, ignored, and forgotten women to be heard. By hastening to Hull House in search of this monstrous infant, they were rushing for a chance to win the respect of their husbands, children, and neighbors, to seize the spotlight for a moment before slipping back into a painful obscurity:

> had been claimed by the forces of evil, his merely reputed presence had power to attract to Hull House hundreds of women who had been humbled and disgraced ...

Though most accounts of the Devil Baby story begin and end at Hull House, others have speculated that the baby was taken out of the house and sent by the humanitarian Addams to a more isolated home, perhaps even the Waukegan retreat house which she founded on the North Shore.

Today, among believers in the existence of a so-called Devil Baby of Hull House, there continues a debate between those who believe that the baby was just that-an earthly manifestation of diabolical origin-and those convinced that the child was, sadly but simply, a deformed infant brought to Hull House by a destitute mother. Believers in the second likelihood also assume that the child either died at Hull House or was sent from public scrutiny to a quieter shelter outside the city.

Whether or not a baby, deformed or demonic, was ever brought to Hull House, belief in the fact has remained fierce. The widespread popularity of the Hollywood film, Rosemary's Baby, which legend holds was inspired by the Hull House story, has proven that the appeal of the tale is hardly provincial, though local accounts persist of an evil little mug that glares out of the upstairs window, as do reports of foggy upper windows and feelings of unease.

Adding to the building's mystery have been the paranormal reports of so many visitors over the years, who claim that not only the house is haunted but the garden between the original house and the dining hall built by Addams after she moved in. Mediums and clairvoyants claim there is a "portal" or interdimensional doorway in this area, possibly opened by Native Americans when white encroachment forced them from early Chicago.

Others have spoken about an "abortion graveyard" here in the garden, as Addams was an early advocate of birth control and abortion, which she and other progressives held to be tools of empowerment for women. Whether abortions were done at Hull House we do not know, but it is certainly possible given the radically progressive nature of Addams and many of her staff.

During her lifetime, Addams did what she could to prevent this "haunting" of Hull House. Soon after the phenomenon, she seized the opportunity to proselytize on the wretched state of women's lives, sharing her visitors' stories with the readership of the Atlantic Monthly in October 1916 and emphasizing her belief that the old women who came to visit the Devil Baby believed that the story "would secure them a hearing at home… and as they prepared themselves with every detail of it, their old faces shone with a timid satisfaction."

These days, as busloads of ghost hunters eyeball Hull House hoping for a glimpse of a gruesome little face, a misty window, or a filmy form on the staircase, Jane Addams must turn often in her grave, disgusted by what she felt was a foul and fantastic fairy tale. Yet even the realistic progressivist was not altogether grounded in "modern" convictions. During her own administration of Hull House, Addams engaged in at least one superstition of her own: placing pails of water at the threshold of her bedroom . . . to keep the ghosts away.

Intriguingly, one obscure version of the Devil Baby story ties it to the urban legend known as the "Devil in the Dancehall," an incidence of which was alleged to have occurred in Chicago's Bridgeport neighborhood, a short distance from Hull House, in Chicago's Bridgeport neighborhood, home of the Daley family for generations and still an unmoving landmark of old Chicago politics, social relations, architecture, and economics.

Here, on street corners and front stoops, in barber shops and beauty parlors, and in the ubiquitous corner taverns, talk abounds, spanning many topics, many opinions, many generations. Listeners will be engaged by the most amazing of memories, including those recalling one unforgettable neighborhood night: the night the Devil came to dance.

Local tradition remembers it on a Saturday night in an old ballroom just west of Loomis Street on Archer Avenue. A young unescorted woman became enchanted by a mysterious and dashing stranger whose acquaintance she had made on the dance floor. As they whirled to the music with the other local couples, the girl happened to glance at the exceptionally deft feet of her partner.

Responding to her subsequent scream, the neighborhood men, assuming the stranger had made inappropriate advances, immediately pursued her escort who had quickly fled from the scene. When he was cornered near a second-floor window, the stranger alarmed the crowd by refusing to fight, instead leaping from the ledge to the pavement below. When the onlookers rushed to the window to observe his fate, they were amazed to discover that the man had landed squarely on his feet.

As he bolted across Archer, the furious crowd rushed from the building and after the fugitive. Once outside, however, the onlookers discovered the real reason for the young woman's scream. Imbedded in the concrete, in the spot where the stranger had landed, was a single but unmistakable hoofprint.

The legend of "The Devil in the Dancehall," according to folklore expert Jan Harold Brunvand, is a popular one in the Mexican and Latin-American traditions. As with all folk legends, the versions are many, but the story line is the same. A person at a dance, usually a young girl, dances with a charming stranger who turns out to have horse's hooves or chicken claws, the Hispanic versions of the rather generic American perception of diabolic "hooves." When the stranger's identity is thus discovered, he disappears in a puff of smoke, leaving only the smell of sulfur and an unconscious young woman as mementos.

One of the stories that lives on in the Rio Grande Valley is the notorious tale of the girl who danced with the devil.

The "Devil at the Disco" or the "Devil at the Dance" folktale centers around a young girl who liked to go out on the weekends, and, despite her parents' warnings about not going out during Holy Week, she ended up at Boccaccio's –*the* most popular nightclub in McAllen – the night of Good Friday in 1979.

Amid the dazzling lights and pop music, a tall, handsome stranger walked in, elegantly dressed and ready to sweep the girl off her feet. Literally.

"At midnight sharp, this extremely well-dressed young man wearing a cape comes in and walks straight to her and asks her to dance," recounts Dr. Mark Glazer, a retired UTRGV legacy professor of anthropology.

"They dance, they start to go around and around, and they start moving up and up until they reach the roof. He then drops her and disappears. When he disappears, the smell of sulfur is left behind."

That smell of sulfur? The devil's trademark.

Though variations of the story change, it was discovered that, as the couple danced, the handsome stranger, assumed to be the devil, had one hoof and one chicken's talon in place of feet.

Chaos ensued. In some versions of the story, the girl had burns where the devil touched her. Other variations claim the girl died on the spot, while others say the girl went crazy and is still alive and living in the Valley – still waiting for her handsome stranger to return.

When he wrote The Vanishing Hitchhiker, his classic first volume on urban folk legends, Brunvand had found no evidence that this legend had made its way into Anglo-American culture. For over half a century, however, the testaments of Bridgeport residents have proven otherwise.

THE ST. VALENTINE'S DAY MASSACRE

Crime buffs eager for a tour of Chicago's gangland attractions are often disappointed by the city's lack of preserved locations. Many of the most notorious sites in the history of Chicago organized crime no longer exist, leaving no evidence but memories of the madness with which they were connected. Gone, for example, is Big Jim Colosimo's restaurant at 2128 South Wabash Avenue where the owner prided himself both on his smoothly-run empire of vice and the "500,000 yards of Spaghetti Always on Hand." Also gone is Sharbaro and Co. Mortuary, 708 N. Wells Street, which hosted two of the biggest funerals in gangland history: one in November 1924, when Dion O'Bannion was carried out the front door in a $10,000 casket; the other in October 1926, after Hymie Weiss was gunned down on the sidewalk across from Holy Name Cathedral.

The Four Deuces Saloon, now a vacant lot at 2222 S. Wabash, long ago welcomed Al Brown from Brooklyn to his first Chicago job as the bouncer who would become Alphonse Capone. Later, the Lexington Hotel at 2135 S. Michigan Avenue would serve as the seat of Capone's crime kingdom. Alas, that palace, along with Capone's own fifth floor suite, has also been demolished in recent years.

---

17   *Chicago Daily News* 1929

For organized crime enthusiasts, however, more missed than any of these is the warehouse which stood at 2122 N. Clark Street, where on Valentine's Day 1929, one of the most gruesome multiple homicides in gangland history was committed.

The building nearly eluded description: a one-story red brick structure, 60 feet wide and 120 feet long, tucked between two four-story buildings that in 1929 somewhat towered over the S-M-C Cartage Company garage between them. On the morning of February 14, a sordid group was gathered inside in retreat from a typical snowy Chicago morning. Ex-safecracker Johnny May, having been hired as an auto mechanic by the notorious gang leader, George "Bugs" Moran, was stretched out under a truck fixing a wheel. Living out of a slipshod apartment, May was grateful for the 50 bucks a week he got from Moran to support his wife, six children, and a dog named Highball, who happened to be at work with him that morning, tied to the axle of the truck.

Huddled around a percolating coffee pot on an electric hotplate, shivering in their overcoats and hats, were another half-dozen assorted characters, including Frank and Pete Gusenberg, who were, per Moran's orders, awaiting a truck-full of hijacked whiskey from Detroit. Moran himself was late for the 10:30 a.m. rendezvous. It was a little after the appointed time when he finally ventured out into the 15 below zero cold with Ted Newberry, a gambling concessionaire, headed towards the garage. The Gusenbergs were antsy, anxious to get started on their own part of the scheme, driving two empty trucks back to Detroit to meet a haul of smuggled Canadian whiskey. Their companions, however, were carefree, having been summoned by Moran merely to help unload the trucks when they arrived. Among the harder hearts-Moran's brother-in-law, James Clark; financial whiz, Adam Heyer; and newcomer Al Weinshank-was Reinhardt Schwimmer, a wanna-be of sorts and a young optometrist who had glommed onto Moran after befriending the gang leader at their mutual home, the Parkway Hotel. After that meeting, Schwimmer frequented the North Side warehouse hangout for the thrill of illicit companionship.

None of the group suspected that a police car had pulled up outside the building or knew that Moran, spotting the car upon his approach, had hightailed it back to the Parkway. While Moran's men whiled away the time under the light of a single naked bulb, four men emerged from the car outside, two in police uniforms and two in civilian clothes. The landlady of a neighboring rooming house watched as the men entered the building, then gasped at the clattering explosion of sound that followed a few moments later.

Soon after, four figures emerged, two marched at gunpoint by the two policemen, amid the clamor of a barking dog. After the car pulled away from the curb and headed down Clark Street, neighbors concerned over the still-howling dog, sent a man in to check on the animal. He remained inside only a few moments before reappearing to report on the scene inside.

Moran's men had been lined up against the rear wall of the garage and sprayed by machine guns in careful swoops of fire which targeted first their heads, then their chests, and finally their stomachs. Despite the shower of death, May and Clark had lived, but with their faces nearly blown off by close-range shotgun blasts. Remarkably, Frank Gusenberg had also survived. When Detective Sweeney arrived at the massacre scene, he recognized the face of his boyhood friend on the body of the bullet-riddled Gusenberg. With 14 bullets in his body, Frank had crawled 20 feet from the blood-soaked rear wall, from where he was taken to Alexian Brothers Hospital. There, upon Gusenberg's revival, Sweeney would repeat the question he'd first posed in the garage: "Frank, in God's name what happened? Who shot you?" only to receive Gusenberg's famously hard-boiled response, "Nobody shot me." Still urged by Sweeney to reveal the killers, Gusenberg instead spat out his last words: "I ain't no copper."

But while the law was temporarily baffled as to the source of such brutality, Bugs Moran immediately named its orchestrator. Upon hearing the news of the gruesome deed, he flatly proclaimed, "Only Capone kills like that."

In fact, Al Capone was at that moment in Florida, playing host at a lavish Miami resort. When questioned by one of his guests about his involvement in the Chicago tragedy, Capone curiously but firmly responded that "the only man who kills like that is Bugs Moran." Of the two testimonies, Moran's was right on. Capone had been the brains behind the bloodbath. While some later stories differed on the names of the gunmen, the core team was comprised of Capone's standard slate of executioners.

In 1945, the front of the S-M-C garage was turned into an antique shop by a couple oblivious to the property's infamy. Unfortunately, their doorway was visited more often by crime buffs than by antiquers, the former of which came to the garage in droves from all over the world and eventually forced the disgusted couple to abandon their venture. Later, in the late 1960s, the building was demolished and the 417 rear wall bricks hauled away by George Patey, a Canadian businessman who first built them into a wall of his nightclub, then envisioned them as wonderfully lurid souvenirs, which he promptly sold off to crime buffs. According to rumors, however, anyone who purchased one of the S-M-C bricks was besieged by bad luck, in the form of illness, financial or family ruin, or any of a variety of other maladies. The very structure seemed to have been infused with the powerful negativity of that Valentine's Day.

As did the site.

Five trees dot the otherwise nondescript space, the middle one marking the spot where the rear wall once stood. To this day, an occasional stroller along Clark Street will report hearing violent screams ringing off the fenced-off lot once occupied by the garage that is now part of a nursing home's front lawn. Jason Nhyte and Dave Black of Supernatural Occurrence Studies repeatedly visited the site to investigate well-known allegations of its haunting. On Valentine's Day of 1998 Dave Black finally captured a photograph of an anomalous ring of mist, the only known photograph of its kind from the site.

Moreover, those walking dogs are often puzzled by their pets' curious reaction to this stretch of sidewalk, as their animals either growl or bark furiously at the apparent nothingness or whimper as they crouch away from the iron fence.

Perhaps dogs, known to be more psychically sensitive than most of their masters, are reacting to something unknown to their human companions, a massive surge of energy produced and sustained at the site by the impact of the massacre; a vision of Highball, forever snapping his leash in the aftermath of the bloodbath; or the ringing in their painfully acute ears of the rat-a-tat of Capone's heartless love song, hand-delivered long ago to an unwilling gathering of wallflowers.

Alphonse Capone left long shadows on the city he owned. Some say that, in light of continuing corruption at City Hall and the shady dealings of police brass, Capone still owns Chicago more than half a century after his decidedly inglorious death. Haunted in their own way by the villain's indestructible and international image, recent administrations have led aggressive but covert campaigns to eradicate from the city's face all traces of Capone's kingdom. To the chagrin of crime buffs, Chicago razed, one by one, the accidental memorials to the town's gangland glory, from the Four Deuces Saloon where the Brooklyn boy got his Chi-town start to the garage where he waged the battle that won his war: the S-M-C Cartage Company garage on north Clark Street, where Capone's men carried out the St. Valentine's Day Massacre of 1929.

In life, Capone stayed always at the center of the action, most notably at the old Lexington Hotel south of Chicago's Loop. From his suite on an upper floor, he ran Chicago and ruined lives. Though he died in his Florida home, where he'd been when he'd "heard" of the St. Valentine's Day Massacre, it was here that he should have returned to spend his eternity. And he did, at least for a while. From the time of his death until the demolition of the building in the 1990s, passers-by on south Michigan Avenue often spotted a glimmering form moving from room to room in the windows of the abandoned hotel. When talk arose of the landmark's razing, more than a few natives, convinced of Al's presence at the place, wondered where Capone would go. Though some modern-day fans hoped he would resurface elsewhere in Chicago, most prayed for a speedy trip, Heaven- or Hell-ward, for the hoodlum, tired of the sordid Chicago his memory continued to foster.

Soon after the destruction of the Lexington, the owners of Capone's old pleasure boat, *Duchess III*, experienced a lively new flurry of supernaturalism on the already haunted yacht. Those familiar with the craft's history wondered at the activity: had the boat's erstwhile captain returned to the only helm he had left?

During his reign, Al Capone spent his off-hours indulging in luxurious leisure, hunting and fishing with often great success. The *Duchess III*, named after a particularly enchanting prostitute in Al's employ, was only one in a collection of cruisers that Capone kept up. After a decade of use, the pristine craft gradually deteriorated. When new owners began a tedious restoration of the darkly historic *Duchess*, they discovered a few extra hands-on board: the yacht was definitely haunted. In fact, so frequent are the visual and audio apparitions in one below-deck area, it has been christened the "ghost room." The owners and their guests have heard a baby's wails and a woman's cries and have even viewed a phantom replay of a tempestuous scene: a male figure grabbing a baby from a woman's arms and throwing the child overboard.

Along with the troubling specters, a number of individuals have confronted intense "cold spots" on board the *Duchess*: freezing pockets of air that paralyze the body, even in sweltering heat.

Even from the shore, the ship confounds. Time and again, local fishermen have watched a flame-like light moving among the portholes of the *Duchess* when she was supposedly deserted.

Capone himself was no stranger to the supernatural. Fifteen years before his death, he contacted psychic Alice Britt, pleading for her help in ridding him of a very personal phantom: the ghost of St. Valentine's Day Massacre victim, and Bugs Moran's brother-in-law, James Clark, who Capone claimed had been harassing him since Clark's brutal death.

For nearly 20 years, friends and bodyguards witnessed the disturbing interplay between Al and his unseen oppressor. Day and night Capone's weeping could be heard, punctuated by mad begging to be left alone. Sympathetic skeptics reason that the syphilis Al battled in his later years caused his insanity. Surely, they say, this is the source of the "ghost" he imagined: Capone's own guilt made monstrous by disease-inspired hallucinations.

But if this is true, Capone certainly would have been mad, the guilt of the hundreds of deaths he commissioned peopling his mind with an army of apparitions. James Clark was, then, only a representative illusion—or very real indeed.

THE BIOGRAPH THEATER

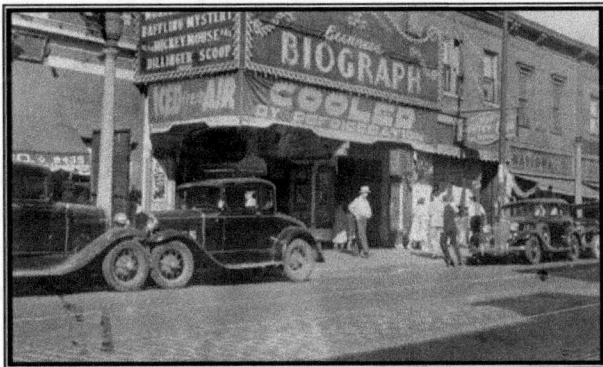

The focal point in the thrilling tale that created one of the city's most famous and favorite ghosts, the Biograph Theater on north Lincoln Avenue welcomed a very special guest on a hot July night in 1934 to his last picture show: John Dillinger, christened by his pursuers as Public Enemy Number One.

That evening, Dillinger left the theater accompanied by Anna Sage, the legendary "Lady in Red" and a favorite prostitute, Polly Hamilton, with whom he had been holed up with at her 2420 N. Halsted Street apartment. At that point, the infamous criminal met his long-avoided end in a narrow alleyway just steps from the theater doors. The bullet fired through the back of his neck by FBI Agent Charles Winstead had been a long time coming. Congratulations poured into the Chicago Police Department and U.S. government agencies from around the world. For while Dillinger's international renown had been quickly won, he made it unforgettable by being impossibly hard to nab.For four months, Melvin Purvis, the soft-spoken head of Chicago's FBI agents, had lived and breathed the chase for the Indiana-born gangster, desperate to snag him before Purvis' critics could oust him in favor of "a more experienced man." In hot pursuit of his prey, Purvis had lived from tip to tip, leading his agents in a foiled attempt to surround the scoundrel at a State Street and Austin cafe, an impressive but ill-fated

18   The Biograph Theater in 1934. FBI photograph (Public Domain)

attack on Dillinger's North Woods hideout at Sault St. Marie, and the infamous confrontation at Wisconsin's Little Bohemia Lodge, in which FBI agents recklessly injured two civilians and killed a third. It was here, too, that George "Baby Face" Nelson reportedly killed Special Agent W. Carter Baum, prompting FBI Chief J. Edgar Hoover to call Nelson a "rat." Yet these near misses with the FBI were only the last stretch of a sensational, though short, career. summary of the "High Points in Life of John Dillinger" was provided by the *Chicago Tribune* on the morning after his fatal shooting. What follows the headline is a catalog of arrests, sentencings, shootouts, and escapes. At the age of 20, Dillinger held up his hometown grocery store in Mooresville, Indiana. Pleading guilty, he was sentenced to serve 10 to 20 years in prison, while his accomplice, pleading not guilty, received a sentence of little more than two years. Bitterly reflecting on this joke of justice, Dillinger spent a quiet eight and a half years planning his revenge on the law. On May 22, 1933, the then-unknown Dillinger was paroled and proceeded to rob three banks in as many months, making off with $40,000. He was incarcerated at Lima, Ohio in September of that same year. When, barely three weeks later, three former fellow inmates invaded the prison and sprung Dillinger, they ushered the convict into a brief but stellar stint as an internationally notorious gangster. His gang would be described after his death as "the most notorious band of outlaws in America, probably the world."

Eluding a police trap in November, the gang pulled off a bank robbery later that month. To celebrate the new year, an unrepentant Dillinger shot and killed police officer William O'Malley in another bank robbery in East Chicago, for which he was arrested in Arizona and sent to Crown Point, Indiana to stand trial. Predictably, he escaped a month later by carving a gun out of soap and blackening it with shoe polish and eluded pursuers for another month. Finding himself at that point in another jam, he shot his way out of a St. Paul police trap on March 31st and made a similar escape from the FBI trap near Mercer, Wisconsin, where he killed two people in the process at the Little Bohemia Lodge. Two months later, police found a Ford V-8 at Roscoe and Leavitt streets treated with a fingerprint-dissolving chemical and with one of the windows smashed out to facilitate shotgunning. Inside the car were a half dozen pop bottles, a baby stroller used to tote tommy guns during getaways, and a matchbook from the Little Bohemia Lodge. There was no doubt about it. Dillinger was in Chicago.

In late June, Dillinger was home again, his gang robbing a South Bend, Indiana bank, wounding four civilians and slaying police officer William P. O'Malley, a close friend of East Chicago's then-police chief, Martin Zarkovich.

In little more than a year, Dillinger had led six major bank robberies, killed two police officers, a civilian, and two FBI agents, escaped imprisonment twice, and eluded or shot his way out of a half-dozen cleverly-laid traps.

Prior to his death, the hardened gangster had been well aware of his streak of fortune and was none too secure about its future continuance. In May 1934, a skittish Dillinger had called his lawyer to discuss the prospect of plastic surgery. On the run from nearly every law enforcement agent in the country, the outlaw yet dared to hope for a new freedom, freedom which might be realized through the alteration of his well-known countenance and the obliteration of his infamous fingerprints. Accustomed to relying on none but himself and his gang for salvation, Dillinger was nonetheless prepared to put his money on one man, a surgeon by the name of Loeser. The gangster felt his trust was well placed, for he and his would-be doctor were birds of a feather: the latter had done time in Leavenworth on a narcotics charge. Sprung from his cage, Loeser was in dire need of funds. In payment for the surgeon's services, Dillinger opened his billfold to the tune of five grand.

On May 27th, the optimistic hood arrived on schedule for the promised procedure, met by his lawyer. In a derelict northside flat, owned by an ex-speakeasy operator, the two passed the night in expectation of the doctor's arrival the next day. When Loeser showed, however, the gangster and his counsel were disturbed to find him accompanied by a pallid and nerve-wracked young assistant. Soothed by the doctor's reassurances, the patient recited his wish list to the attentive Loeser: remove three moles and his giveaway scar; fill in his cleft chin and the bridge of his nose; and, most importantly, nix the damning fingerprints. Agreeing to the changes, Loeser showed Dillinger to a cot, instructed his assistant to administer a general anesthetic, and left the room to prepare for the operation. Placing an ether-soaked towel over Dillinger's nose and mouth, the assistant advised his charge to take some deep breaths. The patient obliged, with dire results. The flustered accomplice- had given the gangster a dangerous dosage and his face proceeded to turn blue. Then, to the young man's horror, Dillinger swallowed his tongue.

Summoned by his assistant's screams, Loeser grabbed his forceps and pulled Dillinger's tongue from his throat. The patient was not breathing. In a ramshackle flat on a quiet Chicago morning, the world's most wanted criminal was dead.

Thoroughly alarmed to action, Loeser worked furiously to restore respiration. After a few moments on the other side, Dillinger was revived, reassured, and re-anaesthetized. The surgery was resumed and completed to the gangster's satisfaction. Ironically, a mere 25 days later, Dillinger's new lease on life was bluntly terminated by a well-placed bullet from the frantic FBI.

At approximately 8:30 in the evening on July 22nd, the surgically-altered outlaw strolled into a screening of "Manhattan Melodrama" at the Biograph Theater on north Lincoln Avenue, observed by no less than 16 police officers and FBI agents, including Melvin Purvis himself. For two hours and four minutes, the watchers waited, one or another occasionally entering the theater to walk the aisles in search of their prey. When Dillinger finally emerged onto the sidewalk, his would-be captors were more than ready, but a little bit wary.

Public Enemy Number One he was, but he looked nothing like the romantic trench-coated antagonist noir that popular culture imagined. Instead, agents beheld a weary moviegoer on a hot summer night, clad in a straw hat, a gray-and-black flecked tie knotted onto a white silk shirt, canvas shoes, and gray summer trousers. Coatless, he appeared unarmed as well and must have undermined the resolve of more than a few of his stalkers, especially in light of his altered features. To Purvis, however, he was unmistakable: 'I knew him the minute I saw him. You couldn't miss if you had studied that face as much as I have.'

As the target strolled south on Lincoln Avenue, he stepped down a curb to a narrow alley entrance. As Dillinger turned down the passageway, a half dozen agents closed in. The moment froze as Dillinger, his back to the pack, instinctively went for a cleverly concealed .38-too late. Four shots were fired, three hitting their mark. Among a swarm of home-bound moviegoers and nearly a score of law enforcement officers, Dillinger went down. Chaos ensued.

According to the *Chicago Tribune*, Dillinger dropped at the feet of Mrs. Pearl Doss, a woman that recognized the fallen man as "Johnnie," a neighbor boy from her Indiana youth. Doss claimed that in that moment of recognition she was close enough to catch his classic last words: "They've got me at last."

A nearby barkeep mistook the victim for his brother-in-law, sending his wife into hysterics. Tradition tells of passers-by running to dip their handkerchiefs in the still-flowing blood, anxious for gruesome souvenirs of the startling event. Struggling for control, Purvis ordered that Dillinger be rushed to nearby Alexian Brothers Hospital. Dead on arrival, Dillinger's body was turned away at the doors. The strange party retired to the hospital lawn to await the deputy coroner.

That night the city awoke, electric. For weeks, Northsiders had been warned by police at the Town Hall and Sheffield district headquarters that the outlaw had been seen in Lakeview, North Center, and Uptown by various witnesses. A March 7th edition of the local Booster newspaper proclaimed:

> *LOOK UNDER YOUR BED. SEARCH YOUR CELLAR.*
> *SHAKE OUT THE MOTHBALLS FROM LAST SUMMER'S*
> *CLOTHES. DILLINGER IS HIDING SOMEWHERE HERE.*
> *AND HE MAY BE HIDING IN YOUR BACKYARD.*

One lifetime North Side resident, my aunt Frances Kathrein, recalled that sweltering July night in 1934, when she and her brothers and sisters lay sleeping on the front-room floor of their second-story flat, hoping for a breath of wind through the screen door. What wafted through that door was not a summer breeze, however, but a sudden sound of commotion on the street outside. Frances' future husband, Norbert, then 13 years old, tore down Cuyler Avenue with a group of newsboys full of papers and cries of "Extra!" and delivering in loud voices the news: "Dillinger's Shot!"

In a report shocking for its day, the *Chicago Tribune* reported on the mob scene at the Cook County morgue, where the line of curiosity-seekers snaked through the building, apparently oblivious to rows of exposed corpses, and stretched down the block outside. The coroner, a man by the name of Walsh, after viewing the crowd "with apparent satisfaction,"[19] posed for photographs with the body. At his instruction, Dillinger's corpse was placed in a basement room behind a glass panel so that the crowds might be allowed to file past for a look at the expired Enemy. The scene was as absurd as might be imagined, and the Tribune presented it in all its brutishness, focusing particular attention on the women in the crowd, who

> pushed forward with massive shoulders and hips. Some of them sighed or groaned with a pretense of horror as they looked at the body, tilted at a 45- degree angle to give a better view. One or two with faces slightly less depraved than the others clucked their tongues and said as they went away: I wouldn't have wanted to see him except that I think it's a moral lesson, don't you? ... One fat blonde woman, after leaving the basement, applied fresh lipstick and, preparing to join the waiting line to have another look, said, 'I'm disappointed. Looks just like any other dead man.'[20]

The Biograph Theater manager declined a chance to speak to the press about the theater's role in the set-up, fearing possible ill-effects on his business. On the other hand, when one reporter, hoping to squeeze some information from Morris Oppenheimer, the proprietor of the bar next door, arrived at the tavern, he found that Oppenheimer had "already paint[ed] a sign, in blood-red letters, proclaiming:

DILLINGER HAD HIS LAST DRINK HERE

In light of the mania following Dillinger's death, it seems almost unbelievable that no unusual phenomena were reported at the shooting site in the immediate months and years that followed. In fact, it was not until the 1970s that passers-by on north Lincoln Avenue began to spot a bluish figure running down the alley, stumbling, falling, and disappearing. Accompanying such sightings were the typical reports of cold spots, feelings of uneasiness, and the sudden unwillingness to use the alley as a handy shortcut to Halsted Street.

---

19   *Chicago Tribune* on Dillinger: viewed with apparent satisfaction article
20   Ibid.

In recent years, while paranormal tales of that alleyway have lapsed, its history and mystery remain. Visitors to the Biograph Theater can examine a diagram on the window of the old box office describing the complex set-up of Dillinger by Melvin Purvis' FBI. Led by the story, they can sit in the seat where Dillinger sat more than 60 years ago and afterwards emerge to walk his last path to the passage still known by older Chicagoans as "Dillinger's Alley." There, just beyond the pool of neon light shed by the theater's brilliant marquee, the imaginative and the perceptive might well wonder about the supernatural survival of that most reluctant of victims.

Dillinger's will to live may continue to inspire us to doubt his death, a doubt that echoes that of Mary Kinder, a friend of Dillinger's. Kinder had certainly read the news about the shoot-out in the alley and had talked with a legion of reporters the next morning about her reaction to the fugitive's demise. Despite the undeniable fact of Dillinger's demise, the girl couldn't help asking, as some still do, "Is it true? Is he dead?"

THE CONGRESS PLAZA

21

One of Chicago's largest hotels, the Congress Plaza, was originally named the Auditorium Annex when it was built to house visitors to the Columbian Exposition—the transformative World's Fair of 1893. The name referenced the Auditorium Theater across Congress Street, an acoustically magnificent structure designed by blockbuster architectural duo Dankmar Adler and Louis Sullivan. The Annex's original North Tower was designed by Clinton Warren, but Adler and Sullivan oversaw its development, including the addition of "Peacock Alley," an ornate marble tunnel which ran under the street, joining the theater and the hotel. Later, in the early twentieth century, the firm of Holabird & Roche designed the South Tower, completing the current structure, which houses more than 800 rooms. The South Tower construction included a magnificent banquet hall, now known as the Gold Room, which would become the first hotel ballroom in America to use air-conditioning. Another ballroom, called the Florentine Room, was added to the North Tower in 1909. These two famous public rooms combined with the Elizabethan Room and the Pompeian Room to host Chicago's elite social events of the day.

---

21   The Congress Plaza Hotel (left) was originally called the Auditorium Annex for the Auditorium Theatre building (right). Today the hotel is recognizable by the neon sign on its roof, visible from Lake Shore Drive. (Library of Congress)

On June 15, 2003, members of the UNITE HERE Local staff at the Congress began a strike after the hotel froze employee wages and revoked key benefits, including health insurance and retirement plans. Through the long months and years, the strikers won countless supporters, their cause garnering momentum around the world. Even future president Barack Obama and Illinois Governor Patrick Quinn walked their picket line, while the skeleton crew that continued to punch the clock was reported to have pocketed wages of more than thirty percent below the national standard. The strike went on to claim the fortunate honor as the longest hotel strike in history, leaving in its wake a hotel haunted by pulled proms, boycotted conventions and an estimated loss of 700 million dollars in revenue.

And many, many ghosts.

Indeed, the ghosts of the Congress are everywhere. And no wonder. Grover Cleveland, William McKinley, Teddy Roosevelt, William Howard Taft, Woodrow Wilson, Warren Harding, Calvin Coolidge, and Franklin Roosevelt all made the Congress their base of operations while in Chicago, leading to the hotel's longtime moniker, "The Home of Presidents." In 1912, President Theodore Roosevelt announced his new "Bull Moose" platform in the Florentine Ballroom, and in 1932 the hotel served as headquarters for Franklin Roosevelt and his hopeful Democratic party. A few years later, Benny Goodman broadcast his wildly popular radio show from the hotel's Urban Room, a posh nightclub that drew the city's most coveted clientele, and in 1971, President Richard Nixon addressed the Midwest Chapters of the AARP and National Retired Teachers Association, speaking before no less than three thousand members and guests in the hotel's Great Hall. For years Al Capone played cards every Friday night in a meeting room overlooking Grant Park, and rumors abound (though most certainly false) that he even owned the Congress for a while. What is true is that Jake "Greasy Thumb" Gusik phoned Capone in Palm Island, Florida, from a phone in the Congress Plaza . . . before and after the St. Valentine's Day Massacre.

But the ghosts of the Congress are not generally those of headline-grabbers. Rather, they are wisps of memory, glimmers of the hundreds of thousands of ordinary guests who have glided through its halls for more than a century, often embroiled in personal drama, heartache and tragedy.

Endless, it seems, are the stories that echo the tale of James Kennedy, a New York man who checked in, alone, in May of 1910. He went to his room, cut the dry cleaners identification tags out of his clothes, burned his papers, walked to the Lake and shot himself. Later that same year, an insurance salesman--Andrew Mack--called on a friend at his Congress Plaza hotel room before also walking to the Lake and apparently drowning himself at the foot of Van Buren Street. There was the salesman who threw himself down an elevator shaft, the drifter who jumped off the roof of the north tower and the troubled family man who hanged himself from a cupboard hook.

In the summer of 1916, mining investor Morse Davis and his wife were believed to have formed a suicide pact when Davis was found dead in their Congress hotel room 312 of cyanide poisoning. His wife was also at death's door but alive. She claimed they had taken the cyanide by accident, having confused it with Epsom salts. A few days later, however, --broke and staying at St. Mary's Mission house on Peoria street--she tried to throw herself out a third story window and was promptly sent to a psychiatric hospital.

In August of 1939, Adele Langer, a Prague native, threw her young sons, Karel and Jan, from a thirteenth-floor window in the Congress Plaza. Langer's widower described the family's despair at being forced to flee Nazi influence in their homeland, leaving behind home and family.

In August of 1950 a guest shot a Congress employee and then himself when the staff member came into the guestroom to collect on a $104 hotel bill for the jobless and distraught boarder.

In May of 1966, Rockford attorney Frederick Haye was found naked and strangled with his shirt, his wrists and feet bound with his own socks.

Accidents, too, have left their mark here. In 1904, an elevator operator at the Auditorium Annex fell seventy feet to the subfloor, dying on impact. In July of 1926 a Galesburg woman, Mrs. Harriet Harrison, staying at the Congress with her husband before a planned European excursion, took a wrong step and plunged six stories down an elevator shaft to the hotel basement.

Since 1989, I have participated in more than 3 dozen investigations of the Congress Plaza, documenting no fewer than 47 distinctively haunted rooms and at least two ballrooms, as well as common areas such as employee workrooms and public guest areas. The sheer variety of phenomena reported and experienced at this massive structure is mind-boggling. Truly, there seems to be no end to the historic tragedy or of its supernatural manifestations.

The Florentine Room, an ornately painted ballroom, was originally also used as a roller rink when the hotel opened to World's Fair visitors in the 1890s. Security guards say that, on their wee-hour rounds, cheerful organ music can still be heard from outside the locked doors, as well as the sound of old wooden skate wheels against the wooden floors. The piano is known to play by itself, and a woman may be heard screaming outside a staff door on the east side of the room. The women's restroom is likewise haunted by a female presence, who appears in the mirrors, staring at the living and following them out down the hallway.

In the lavish Gold Room—a hotspot for Chicago wedding receptions—bride and groom are often chilled by photographers' photos. Those snapped around the grand piano tend to develop with one or more people missing from the pictures, and the doors tend to be found unlocked no matter how often they are securely shuttered.

In the South Tower, there is the phantom who lingers at the fifth-floor passenger elevator, where moaning is frequently heard by guests awaiting its arrival. The third-floor hallways are home to a one-legged man, often reported to the front desk by guests who think a vagrant has found his way inside. One former hotel operator who worked the property in the 1940s remembers a resident with a wooden leg who always had a big smile and a big tip, who suffered a heart attack at breakfast during his residency and died.

Also in the South Tower, a young boy of about ten has been a prolific presence, running up and down the halls in knee breeches and high button boots. Guessing at his identity, some tie him to one of the many families who made their homes at the hotel in years gone by, and the all-too-common deaths from then-incurable illnesses like tuberculosis and pneumonia.

As for sleeping rooms, only one guest room in the South Tower is reported to be haunted: Room 905, where constant phone static has bedeviled guests for years.

But the North Tower? That's a different story.

In Room 474 a once-resident judge eternally changes the channels on his cherished television set. In Room 759 another erstwhile resident pulls the door shut from inside when guests try to enter. It is said that he was an elderly gentleman—a longtime resident--whose son had come to take him to a nursing home many years ago. Wanting to stay put at the hotel, he mustered the strength to try to keep his son (and security guards) from opening the door. Even now he remains, determined to live at the Congress forever.

And then there are the rooms that that I promised the management not to number: the room where the pictures on the wall rotate 360 degrees before the eyes of astonished residents; the room where an impromptu exorcism was held, on some unidentified Chicago winter's night not so long ago, before the victim was moved to a local convent. There is the room fled by two Marines in 1989, running through the lobby in their boxer shorts at 3 a.m., with the later explanation that a towering black figure had entered the room from the closet and approached their beds, and the room where a woman slit her wrists in the bathtub after a night on Rush Street in the 1970s, who is said to still be glimpsed during the night by weary boarders.

And then there is THE room.

Rumors have long flown that it was a room here at the Congress Plaza that partly inspired writer Stephen King to create his short story, 1408, a gripping tale of a professional—and skeptical—ghost hunter who meets his match in a mysterious hotel room (1408) said to be too haunted to lease. Unbelieving, the young man convinces the hotel's manager to let him have the room for a night, though the previous tenants all took their own lives during their stays in it. The real-life 1408 was always believed to exist on the Congress's most haunted floor: the 12th floor of the older North Tower. Some point to a room which is padlocked and say that's the one. Others say it's the one that's been boarded up. Still others claim you can't even place it anymore: it's been papered over to remove any sign that it was ever there. This room does, in fact, remain. But it's not on the 12th floor.

If it still had a number, the room would be--believed it or not-- number 666. At some point in time, the spot where this room's door should be drywalled over, a piece of baseboard patched in to connect the wood where the doorway once stood. The lintel above the old doorway is, indeed, still quite visible. Some have ventured that this room was simply put out of use because of its stigmatized number, but there is definitely more to this story. Though no staff member claims to remember why this room was sealed off forever, window washers tell us it was closed up with the furniture still inside, almost as if even the objects in the room were believed to be cursed.

Over the past thirty years, I've had my own harrowing moments at the Congress Plaza. There was the morning I was awoken by the sound of the shower blasting full force, steam filling the bathroom, though I could get barely a trickle and little warmth when I'd tried to take a bath. There was the night my worst fear as a ghost hunter came true: the sheets and blankets were peeled off me by unseen hands as I slept. Then came the Night of Incessant Knocking, as we came to christen it: More than a dozen times through the night, someone rapped three times on our door, but no one stood by. And there was the night my daughter and I were kept awake, chillingly, by the sound of two men whispering at the foot of our bed: "Are they still awake?"

Incredibly, I discovered in recent years that the hotel operating on the site of the Congress before it was built was also known to be haunted!

By the year of the Great Fire, the U.S. Custom House had operated in today's Printer's Row area for a little over fifteen years. The building housed not only the Collector of Customs but the equivalent of the IRS, the Steamboat Inspector, the U.S. Commissioner, the U.S. Marshal and the postal clerks' offices. On the top floors were the federal courts, district attorney and clerks of court. Wryly, the Custom House was one of several so-called "fireproof" buildings that would be decimated by the Great Fire in 1871.

After the Great Fire destroyed the Custom House, the U.S. government moved their various orphaned offices into Congress Hall, an old hotel at Michigan Avenue and Congress Boulevard which had survived the Fire. A decade later, the building would be razed to build the new Auditorium Annex Theater (today's notoriously haunted Congress Plaza Hotel), for visitors to the World's Fair of 1893. But just after the Fire, by December of 1871, the old hotel site was already known as haunted.

Soon after their tenancy began, stories of phantom footfalls and other strange sounds began to be reported by government workers, and—not long after-- a chilling story surfaced to explain the strange events, which were tied to a porter who had worked in the old Congress Hall Hotel.

The dead porter's former roommate told the tale of an evening when his friend had gone out to bathe in the Lake. When the porter came back later, his friend saw that he was pale and distressed, and he got into bed with his clothes on, falling asleep without a word.

In the morning, the porter was gone. Later that afternoon, while his friend stood chatting with an associate in the lobby, the body of the porter was brought in on a stretcher. He had drowned the evening before in Lake Michigan.

Not long after the man's death, the housekeepers at Congress Hall Hotel began to report strange noises in his former room and a feeling of unease. Then, one night about three months after the drowning, several people saw the dead man appear, dressed in soaking wet clothing, standing in the doorway leading to the yard of the hotel. The night watchmen at the hotel also reported hearing the sound of walking between 9pm and midnight most nights, and the engineer claimed to have heard someone snoring in his room when he was quite alone. On another occasion he went into the basement, where the porter used to nap on his duty nights, and found the chairs turned upside down, inkstands overturned, and papers and other items strewn about the room.

Another night watchman was driven nearly crazy, reporting that he was constantly followed by phantom footsteps while making his rounds, the footfalls walking when he walked and stopping when he stopped.

Today the site where the Congress Hall Hotel once stood is occupied by our looming Congress Plaza Hotel, known as one of the most haunted hotels in the world and—for my money—the most haunted building in Chicago. Myriad spirits roam these halls, the victims of so many tragedies that occurred here over many, many years, including those of numerous accidental and purposeful drownings in the lake. Whether the porter who suffered here so many years ago is part of today's gathering of ghosts is anyone's guess.

Whatever the beliefs of others, my own experiences have firmly rooted this enigmatic spot at the pinnacle of my "Most Haunted." Escorting in thousands of tour guests of these 15 years, I have observed that, whether they walk in believing or not, most who enter the Congress today are struck by a peculiar feeling: something "not quite right," something "menacing" or "sinister" as it's variously described. Most leave agreeing that they would rather be alone almost anywhere but in the hallways of this storied monument to Chicago's troubled past, full of sorrow and secrets, with always room for one more.

DEATH'S ALLEY

22

Chicago is a dear friend to disaster. From the 1812 massacre on the Lake Michigan dunes to the 1915 capsizing of the Eastland steamer on the Chicago River (which we'll visit shortly), to the crash of Flight 191 in the spring of 1979, the city has exchanged lives for infamy time and time again, establishing Chicago as an unlucky town indeed. In particular, fire has battled the town's heart an astonishing number of times, marking the passage of decades with blazing reminders of the fallibility of our grandest plans. From pre-founding infernos that reduced whole blocks to cinders, to the infamous fire of 1871, to the unthinkable fire that, in 1958, ended the lives of more than 90 children at Our Lady of the Angels School, fire has been to Chicago an enemy, always waiting around the next corner, eager for heartache and headlines.

Despite the reaping of lives, many of them young, and the destruction of incalculable property, fire has not only destroyed but created. Perhaps the most famous example of this idea is the plan of Chicago itself, the way to which was opened by the wholesale destruction of the city by the Great Fire. In fact, a number of years ago, the City of Chicago formally thanked Catherine O'Leary for keeping the cow that started it all. It was because of that fire, they said, that Chicago, with its grid system and great vistas, is as beautiful and sensible as it is today. More soberly, the Our Lady of the Angels fire inspired fast and sweeping changes in fire

---

22   The Iroquois Theater after the fire. (Library of Congress)

safety codes around the country, as did another, early Chicago inferno: the devastating 1903 fire at the old Iroquois Theatre.[23]

December 30, 1903, found thousands of Chicago children in the throes of leisure. Christmas had come and gone, but this was only Wednesday, and five days remained before the start of school. Ahead lay the New Year's festivities and, for many, days on the town with siblings, cousins, and friends, the groups of cheerful youngsters snaking through the Loop, headed up by weary mothers and aunts.

Turn-of-the-century Chicago was nothing to sniff at; the sights and sounds of its bustling downtown district were enough to hold the most insatiable adolescent in awe of its sheer variety. The usual fare consisted of enormous department store windows, packed with untold goods, street vendors hawking their own wares, a never-ending throng of people clad in all manner of dress and rushing to a thousand appointments, a crush of horses and wagons, and above it all, the thundering elevated train, carrying carloads of passengers over the crush of life below.

But today was even better. For a Christmas holiday treat, nearly 2,000 schoolchildren and their chaperones were due at a special matinee performance of Mr. Blue Beard, starring popular comedian Eddie Foy. The venue was the new Iroquois Theatre, a peach of a theatre that had opened only five weeks earlier on Randolph Street. Built like a rock with the latest in safety equipment, the palace-like lobby elicited many an ooh and aah from the people who piled in that December afternoon. They would be the last accolades that the Iroquois would hear.

The first act of the upbeat musical passed without incident, the audience delighting at the antics of the cast, the luxury of the surroundings, and the impressive orchestra and lighting effects. Then as the second act forged ahead, disaster crept in.

Unnoticed by the audience, a light to the left of the stage area flashed, setting a painted drape on fire that swiftly carried the flame into the space above the performers, igniting the top of the fabric backdrops. Without warning, the blazing drapery crashed down, setting on fire the

---

23   An excellent account of the Iroquois Theatre Fire many be found in David Cowan's *Great Chicago Fires* as well as the book, *Tinder Box* by Anthony P. Hatch. The website, IroquoisTheater.com is invaluable for researchers of the fire and anyone interested in Chicago or fire history.

costume of at least one performer, who rushed offstage in a panic. As the stunned audience blindly rushed out, Eddie Foy attempted to stop the disorderly retreat. With mild success, Foy urged the crowd to remain calm. But when the actors opened a stage door to escape, the draft sent the existing fire blazing, and panic flared, too.

An asbestos curtain had been installed in the "fireproof" theater, but when crew members tried to lower it against the fire, it jammed several feet from the stage floor. Not long after the snafu, part of the stage collapsed. Then, to the horror of all present, the lights went out.

Twenty-seven exits had been designed for the Iroquois, but many had been locked against nonpaying guests. Others were hidden by curtains so as not to spoil the elegance. The stampede of people, the horror of the pitch-blackness, and the lack of available exits combined to create one of the grisliest scenes ever encountered by firefighters anywhere.

By the time they fought their way inside, past a main exit sealed shut by a seven-foot-high wall of corpses, not a living soul remained. Hundreds, most of them women and children, lay, trampled and asphyxiated, behind the main theater doors, doors that opened *inward*.

The Iroquois itself was a shambles of ashes and charred marble, the critically acclaimed "temple of beauty" turned chamber of horrors in a matter of minutes. Over the weeks that followed, more than two dozen with fire-related injuries would join the departed audience members, and hundreds would nurse injuries, some for a lifetime. The indictments that ensued against managers and officials who, in the rush to complete the theater, glossed over inspections and unfinished safety features, offered little consolation to the thousands who lost loved ones in the unspeakable tragedy.

Those who lived tried as best they could to blend back into the lives they had known. Scars, physical, mental, and emotional, made the attempt a brutal struggle. One North Center woman, an Iroquois organist, came away from the disaster alive, but with a face so badly marred that she wore a veil ever after along with the turn-of-the-century costumes she had worn before the fire. Known only as Mrs. Meyers, neighbors would see her well into the 1940s, keeping far from others, outfitted in her somber Gibson Girl attire. On rare daylight outings, she would pause frequently to touch up heavy makeup. In the evenings, neighborhood children followed her stealthily as she made her way, in the safe darkness, to window-shop at Broadway and Lawrence and recall the days when the bustle of the Loop was open to her.

Mrs. Meyers died in 1970, 67 years after the tragedy. With her went one of the last living witnesses to that devastating day on Randolph Street. Theater life there, however, would go on. Sometime after the demolition of the Iroquois, the Oriental Theatre had been built on the same land. Decades passed, and after waning attendance at Loop theaters, the Oriental, too, was shuttered. A massive rehabilitation effort, inspired by Mayor Richard M. Daley's push for the renaissance of the old Randolph Street downtown theater district, threw open the doors on the old Oriental, sparkling again and re-named the Ford Center for the Performing Arts. Yet, while the doors all open outward, and state-of-the-art sprinkler systems stand at the ready, prepared to saturate the tiniest of sparks, something here remains unconvinced of the preparedness of this place.

The alley behind the Ford Center is the same alley that ran behind the ill-fated Iroquois in the waning days of 1903. Though rescuers found at the theater's front the doors barricaded with bodies, the horror out back was, if possible, even worse:

> *The rear alley was a smoking, flaming hell.*
> *Firefighters heard the pounding behind iron-shuttered doors and windows and tried to wrench them open with axes and claw bars. Above them, the unfinished fire escape door suddenly flew open. People, many on fire, were pushed onto the platform that led nowhere but down. Body after body thudded onto the cobblestones.*
>
> *Another fire escape door was pried open, and people were running down it when the door directly underneath was blown open by pent-up heat and gasses. Fire spewing from the door spiraled upward and engulfed people coming down the escape. Firefighters spread black nets, but few of the trapped saw them through the smoke. More jumped and*

survived only because their bodies were cushioned by those
who had leaped before them. [24]

Adding to the death toll in the alleyway were others, mostly women and children, who had attempted to crawl across a makeshift bridge extended by students and workers from the Northwestern University building located across the way, many tumbling to the pile of corpses below. When the mania was over, 125 bodies lay in the space that Chicagoans would forever call "Death Alley."

Bishop Samuel Fallows of St. Paul's Reformed Episcopal Church was among the volunteers at the theater.

"I saw great battlefields of the Civil War, but they were as nothing to this," he said.

Today, the alley behind the fully restored Oriental Theatre/Ford Center for the Performing Arts is usually empty, its narrow passage maneuvered only by the occasional delivery truck, stagehand, or performer, or by a pedestrian grabbing a shortcut to a late appointment.

The void, however, may be deceiving.

Those who do find themselves in "Death Alley" never feel quite alone here, and never quite comfortable.

When I first began investigating Chicago's hauntings there were no stories at all about the Iroquois Fire. I was sure, however, that this site absolutely *must* exhibit phenomena to betray the then largely forgotten disaster that had happened here. And so, I began to visit the site regularly in an attempt to collect evidence of this. I was amazed by what I found.

I soon began to meet stagehands, actors and property managers who attested to the paranormality of the "new" theater space that had been built here, and even—or moreso—that of the alley that ran behind it. They told me of hearing children playing in the alley during performances— sometimes laughing so loudly that a stagehand would be sent out to quiet them... only to find no one there but the laughter still echoing away. They told of actors and staff coming into work through the alley

---

24   "Dead and dying heaped in café" 31 Dec 1903, Thu · Page 4

who would feel little hands try to take theirs, as if a child were trying to walk with them. Others talked about coming out of the stage door and smelling an overpowering smell of smoke as of a house fire—there one minute and utterly gone the next.

When the Broadway smash *Wicked* enjoyed its run here of many years, we began to be flooded with stories from the cast and crew. The property manager told us that, each night before turning the lights out after the show, one could hear children's laughter in the women's bathroom and a toilet flushing. When entering the bathroom, however, no one could be found. The toilet, however (which was *not* a sensory toilet but manually flushed), could be heard with its old tank filling up after a recent flush. He said it was as if little girls were playing at flushing the toilet for fun. Chorus members told of the apparition of a teenaged girl they would see padding up and down the backstage stairs in her bare feet, wearing a sequined leotard—perhaps the phantom of the only cast member who died that day in 1903: a young woman who was part of the tightrope troupe.

He also told us that he had come out to the alley to smoke one night after finally getting a particularly rough show off to a start. He was sitting on the little curb that runs along the theater building and looking down at the cobblestoned alleyway. A woman's voice said to him, "The smoke will kill you." He laughed and looked up, saying, "I know, I know."

There before him was a woman dressed in turn of the 19th century clothing, her full skirts falling to the ground and high, feathered hat framing an ivory face. An instant after he saw her, she vanished.

The theater and alley are not the only places which still ring with residue of the terrible Fire. As the tragedy unfolded, the eighth floor of the Marshall Field & Company Department Store was converted into a hospital where fire victims were bandaged and bound with dish and bath towels from the housewares department. Those who died during treatment were wrapped in sheets and blankets from the bedding department to await the coroner's wagons. The *Chicago Tribune* reported, the day after the disaster, that

> *(t)he west room and employees' sitting room on the eighth*
> *floor were filled within thirty minutes after the work of rescue*

began. Anxious men seeking relatives and friends pushed their way through the crowd. One had heard that his wife and boy had been taken to the store. He found his son safe, but the search for the woman failed.[25]

...One woman, whose two children had not been heard from, went into convulsions, and another half dragged, and half carried in her two children, whose clothing had been almost all torn off of them.

Throughout the years, rumors arose of various employee suicides said to have occurred from the eighth level of the open-air atrium in Marshall Field & Company; coworkers were said to claim that the victims had all spoken of a "heaviness" or depression while working on that floor. Could the use of the floor as a hospital—and morgue—for the Iroquois fire victims have left some kind of deadly impression on the building itself? No one can know for sure, but there seemed to be no stopping the macabre events.

As recently as the summer of 2007, a man entered Macy's just before closing time and—according to employees—purchased a white suit, white hat, white shoes and gloves. He donned his purchases in the men's room, rode the elevator to the eighth floor, and leaped to his death from the atrium rail, ending up splayed across the Coach handbag display. This action led to the installation of thick plexiglass walls above the original railing walls around each atrium floor.

A hospital was founded to memorialize the victims of the Iroquois Fire. In the lobby was installed a bas-relief bronze plaque designed by Lorado Taft, portraying the figure of "Sympathy" leading a procession of humanity. When the Iroquois Emergency Hospital closed, the plaque disappeared. It was found in a basement storage area at City Hall and installed in the lobby of the Cook County building in the Loop. There, in October of 2003, one hundred years after the Iroquois disaster, a fire broke out, killing six people. It was discovered that stairwell doors had been locked, trapping victims inside.

Though the Iroquois Theater Fire is only one of hundreds of ghost stories I have researched and shared over these many years, and though

---

25   Ibid.

I have visited the site with ghost tour guests literally thousands of times, the site of the tragedy and telling of the story never fail to cause me to choke up with emotion. So much so that, many years ago, I stopped taking people there on my tours.

Sometime after, I was invited to speak at a paranormal conference in Sault Ste. Marie, in the Upper Peninsula of Michigan. I am relatively unknown by paranormal enthusiasts outside of Chicago, and few people at the event knew of my work in Chicago, but the organizers thought my lecture—about children in the paranormal—would go over well. I was billed as an "expert" on children and the paranormal, not on Chicago ghosts. Again, few knew me. There was a woman there who was giving readings. She was an empath—someone who picks up on energies surrounding people. I had never met her or even heard her name before, and the conference hadn't started yet. An empath can tap into your own emotions and the emotions of any spirits that may be surrounding you.

I decided to have a reading with her, and she said, "there are many people around you. They live in what looks like an alley, a long dark stretch in a city. They died together in a fire. They want to know why you don't come to see them anymore."

THE EASTLAND DISASTER

26

At 7:30 a.m. on Saturday, July 24, 1915, more than 2,500 passengers had boarded the Eastland steamer, docked between the Clark and LaSalle Street Bridges. The ship was bound for Michigan City, Indiana, where a picnic was to be held for Western Electric employees and their families. Five vessels had been chartered to take the excursion parties on the journey across the lake. The Eastland was the first of these to fill with cheering passengers eager to partake of one of the largest lake excursion parties ever assembled in Chicago. Just after the gangplank had been pulled in, the mooring lines loosed, and the anchor posts pulled, there followed one of the most horrific of all the city's disasters and the worst of all Chicago maritime tragedies.

Though there would be much speculation regarding circumstances of the event, the following account was eventually established as true. As the Eastland prepared to make its way towards the lake, a passing ship caused a sudden interest on one side of the ship's deck, creating a massive rush of bodies toward the diversion. Because the crew had emptied the ballast compartments to allow for more passengers, the result was a sudden and significant imbalance of weight. As the festive

26   Crowds throng the river following the roll over of the Eastland on a summer morning in 1915. (Library of Congress)

crowd waved from the Eastland's deck, the ship simply toppled over. The *Chicago Daily News* surveyed the scene:

> *The river seemed covered with struggling forms. Life preservers were thrown from other boats, lines from shore, boxes and everything movable that would float by frantic spectators on shore, but dozens of those in the water disappeared under the waves or were dragged down by others.*[27]

Yet, the true horror of the moment was at first unseen. The weather had turned foreboding and many hundreds of passengers had already settled inside for the trip across the lake. When the Eastland capsized, they were thrown together into a nearly solid mass which was immediately covered by the inrushing waters of the Chicago River. A few of these struggled to escape their ghastly prison, fighting to reach the upturned side of the vessel. Chicago firefighters and workers from the Commonwealth Edison Company rushed to the scene to chop away the woodworking above the waterline and to bum escape holes through the steel plates of the hull. Initially, bodies were pulled out and resuscitated. All too soon, however, no more lifesaving was possible. The corpses of the drowned were wrapped in sheets and carried to the Roosevelt, another of the excursion vessels docked across the street, to await identification.

By five o'clock that afternoon, nearly 200 bodies were laid out on the floor of the 2nd Regiment Armory at 1054 W. Washington Boulevard. Less than an hour later, a diver who had been recovering bodies since mid-morning went out of his mind and had to be subdued by four policemen. City workers were dragging the river as far south as West Adams Street, having stretched a net across the waterway at West 12th Street to stop the drift of bodies.

At the end of the count, more than 800 passengers had been pronounced dead, among them 22 whole families.

The *Chicago Daily News* listed the "Dead, Injured and Missing" in its afternoon edition, offering what identification could be given to panicked friends and family dreading news of the worst. Too often, the descriptions of the deceased were maddeningly meager, such as "GIRL,

---

27 "919 bodies recovered" Chicago, Illinois · Sunday, July 25, 1915

blue dress" or "MAN, dark suit and white shirt." Others, however, were appallingly familiar, as one which read "WOMAN, about 21 years old; wore three rings, and another marked 'From D.L. to M.F.,' and a locket marked M.F."

The wreckage was eventually cleared, the legalities relatively settled, the living as comforted as they could be by their families, friends, and even the strangers who pitied their losses. But for years thereafter, passers-by on the Clark Street Bridge reported hearing cries of horror emanating from the river and its banks. Many assumed these screams to be those of the vanquished passengers of the ill-fated Eastland or of the hundreds of helpless bystanders who watched them perish.

In recent years, Chicago personality Oprah Winfrey established Harpo Studios in the old 2nd Regiment Armory, which had served as a temporary morgue for the Eastland's victims. According to the experiences of employees, and of Winfrey herself, that grim moment in Chicago history seems to have imbedded itself in the very heart of the building. Winfrey and her staff have apparently reported unusual occurrences and sensations during their time there, which some have attributed to the victims of the Eastland.

Today, wanderers along Wacker Drive may pause a moment at the Clark Street Bridge to cast their eyes down upon the river and to study a plaque commemorating the Eastland dead, the casualties that comprised the worst disaster in Great Lakes history in terms of lives lost. Yet while these words carved in metal are at best silent reminders of that tragic excursion, the cries said to ring across the river are hardly as hushed, and, according to those who have heard them, infinitely more imperious.

RESURRECTION MARY

28

Chet's Melody Lounge sits bravely across the road from Resurrection Cemetery, drawing in a steady stream of locals to shoot the breeze and have a few. For years, regulars pretty much disregarded the Bloody Mary eternally perched at the end of the bar and "The Ballad of Resurrection Mary" once listed among the selections on the jukebox (now replaced by a digital jukebox) just as they have adopted Chicago's most famous phantom as an accepted fact of life. Certainly, the impact of phantom-related folklore on Southwest-side culture, well captured in Kenan Heise's novel, *Resurrection Mary: A Ghost Story*, is indeed most obvious in the cultural prominence of this persistent legend.

But while Mary's legendary spirit has contented itself with the haunting of a brief stretch of Archer Avenue just south of Chicago proper, the image of this elusive personality has thumbed itself into the hearts and history of all Chicago. From the old-timers' still-vibrant accounts of her to the young Chicago rap artists singing about "Rez Mary," this specter's appeal reaches every generation, and with good reason. For nearly a century, travelers along Archer have reported bizarre encounters with a single-minded young woman in a party dress and dancing shoes who seems as real as can be--until she proves herself decidedly otherwise.

---

28   Anna Norkus was killed on the eve of her birthday in 1927. (Photograph courtesy of Frank Andrejasich.)

Typical is the following incident: A young man, out for a night of dancing and drinking, meets an aloof but gorgeous young woman, with whom he dances and tries to socialize. She's cold, both emotionally and physically; her hands are cold as ice. At the end of the evening, she asks for a ride home and slides into the front seat of the car next to the driver. After directing the driver to head north along Archer Avenue, she vanishes from the car just as it passes the gates of Resurrection Cemetery. After some deliberation, the young man, having earlier coaxed the girl's address out of her, decides to drive to her home in Chicago's Back-of-the-Yards neighborhood to see if she turned up all right. The young man is met by a sad looking mother or father at the door who informs him that the girl is dead. She was killed, you see, in an automobile accident some years before.

For many years now, researchers have claimed that the first run-in with Mary occurred in 1936, when the late Jerry Palus spent a whirlwind evening dancing with a lovely young woman at a place called the Liberty Grove and Hall. This was previously thought by researchers like myself to have been a tavern and "dime a dance" place in the South Side's Brighton Park neighborhood, but more recent research by local historian Ray Johnson uncovered the fact that "Liberty Grove" was a name for the area surrounding the old Oh Henry Ballroom, later the Willowbrook, and which (as we've seen) became inextricably connected to the legend of Resurrection Mary. When Palus offered her a ride home with him and his brother she accepted, directing him to drive up Archer Avenue. In front of the gates of Resurrection Cemetery, the young woman said she had to leave him, and that he could not follow her. She left the car, disappearing at the main gate, leaving Jerry—and his bewildered brother—speechless.

I recently discovered, however, an earlier account of a vanishing woman in this area while reading an academic article published in 1942, which in turn referenced a collection of first-hand accounts of "phantom hitchhikers" which had been recorded in Chicago by Professor Archer Taylor before 1933. Taylor is known as one of the most important researchers in folklore, and it was during his time as chair of Germanic Literature and Languages at the University of Chicago that he began to compile his phantom hitchhiker dossier. In fact, the 1942 article seems to have been the first published record of a number of accounts that have been told and retold countless times, not only in Chicago but around the country.

This is one of the stories Taylor recorded:

> *Summit, Illinois (before 1933) The narrator said that she could remember having heard a story before the World's Fair of a woman near the graveyard at Summit. She had stopped people and asked for a ride, had given them a Chicago address and disappeared. When the people called at the address, they learned that the woman had died some time before.*

Summit is the village directly north of Justice, Illinois, where Resurrection Cemetery is located. The graveyard at Summit" is without any doubt Resurrection Cemetery. To be sure, I myself have collected first-hand accounts of a vanishing hitchhiker in which the experiencer told me he saw or picked up the girl in Summit, specifically.

As dance hall encounters with this phantom partner multiplied, they seemed to center on the Oh Henry, and it was here that Mary forged her reputation. But it was on the road itself, in the wee hours of many a dark morning, where she has made her biggest impact.

Resurrection Mary first established herself as a "vanishing hitchhiker" around the same time that Palus first encountered her, when late-night revelers complained to the police that a woman had tried to jump on the running boards of their automobiles as they made their way home along Archer after a night of dancing at the Oh Henry. Other drivers over these many years have been surprised by a beautiful young woman who simply opens the car door and climbs in, directing the driver to proceed up the road and disappearing in the usual way, at the cemetery gates. Some unwitting escorts have even watched her run right through the locked gates and into the darkness beyond. At other times, drivers have watched a woman in a flowing white dress walk along the roadside and then vanish, as if switched off like a light. In some of the most harrowing incidents of all, the woman has been struck while bolting or appearing in front of moving cars. Many drivers and passengers feel the impact of the car hitting the figure, but no body is ever found.

Some researchers speculate that this mystery woman heads for one grave among thousands at the 475-acre burial ground known as Resurrection Cemetery: site number 9819, section MM, that of a young Polish woman, Mary Bregovy. Records indicate that Bregovy was killed in a car accident in 1934, allegedly on her way home from a dance at the Oh Henry. Attempts to link this Mary with the Resurrection legend, however, have yielded far less than satisfactory results.

The evidence begins with the following report, which appeared in the *Chicago Tribune* on March 11, 1934:

> *Girl Killed in Crash. Miss Marie [sic] Bregovy, 21 years old, 4611 S. Damen Avenue, was killed last night when the auto in which she was riding cracked up at [word missing] Street and Wacker Drive. John Reiker, 23, of 15 N. Knight Street, Park N. e, suffered a possible skull fracture and is in the county hospital. John Thoe, 25, 5216 S. Loomis, driver of the car, and Miss Virginia Rozanski, 22, of 4849 S. Lincoln [now Wolcott] were shaken up and scratched. The scene of the accident is known to police as a danger spot. (Thoe) told police he did not see the El substructure.*[29]

A close friend of Bregovy's discovered in the mid-1980s that her late girlfriend's name was being connected with the famous phantom. She went on to describe the fateful day of the accident to an understandably eager reporter. According to Vern Rutkowski, who was interviewed by the *Southtown Economist* on January 22, 1984, the two young women had planned to go shopping on March 10, 1934, near 47th Street and Ashland Avenue. The girls accepted a ride to the popular shopping district from two young men who Bregovy had met, but Rutkowski became irritated with the young men, who she remembered as "wild boys."[30] The girls left the men's car while still some distance from their destination, but not before Bregovy made a date for that night. On their way home, Bregovy criticized Rutkowski's unfriendliness and her disapproval of Bregovy's taste in men. Nonetheless, Rutkowski continued to express her dislike of their latest escorts and cautioned Bregovy about her plans for that night. Determined to keep her date, Bregovy left her girlfriend for the day and went home to 4611 S. Damen Avenue.

---

29   "Girl killed in crash,"
30   Vern Rutkowski "wild boys"

Rutkowski stayed home that Saturday night. She was awakened the next morning by her mother, who informed Rutkowski that Bregovy had been killed in a car accident in the Loop sometime during the evening. Bregovy's parents would learn that, although their daughter had been sitting in the back seat before the time of the accident, she was persuaded by her girlfriend to switch seats, since the latter was not getting along with the driver. Described by Rutkowski as an agreeable and personable young woman, Bregovy was happy to oblige. Because of that congeniality, she was thrown through the passenger window when their car struck one of the I-beams of the elevated structure at Lake Street and Wacker Drive. Three days later, Mary's Polish and Czechoslovakian parents buried their daughter at Resurrection Cemetery.

Since Bregovy was killed in downtown Chicago, it is highly doubtful that this Mary was on her way home from any Southwest-side ballroom and most definitely not on the road outside the legendary cemetery. This Mary, according to the records of the Satala Funeral Home from which Bregovy was buried, was a young factory worker who died in the ambulance on the way to Iroquois Hospital, then on North Wacker Drive.

According to Rutkowski, Bregovy loved to dance. But she also had short, dark hair, a far cry from the flaxen-headed fantasy described through the years by Mary's various escorts. In addition, the late John Satala, the undertaker who prepared Bregovy's body (and who once described Mary as "a hell of a nice girl"),[31] remembered that the eternal attire was, in fact, an orchid-colored dress, not a white one.

Old newspaper interviews with Satala suggest one obvious reason why Bregovy was pegged as the famous phantom, despite having the "wrong" hair color and style, the wrong clothes, and regardless of her dying in the wrong place. Nearly 50 years ago, a caretaker at Resurrection phoned Satala and told him about a "ghost" that had been walking the cemetery grounds. In the caretaker's opinion, the ghost was Bregovy's.[32]

Ultimately, the musing of that one man may have been responsible for the permanent matching of the two Marys in local memory. Yet the transformation of the Bregovy ghost into a "vanishing hitchhiker"

---

31 John Satala, "hell of a nice girl"
32 Ibid

did not gain regional cultural prominence until much later. A general feeling exists that neighborhood old-timers knew of a phantom Bregovy long before the folklore grew to match universal vanishing hitchhiker legends. And so, some skeptics believe it probable that Mary's peers picked up adults' talk about the ghost of Bregovy in Resurrection Cemetery and began to elaborate upon the tale during their drives to and from the old Oh Henry Ballroom, encouraged of course by gin and Saturday night fever. The seemingly countless encounters of generations of witnesses—many not from the area or familiar with Bregovy or even the legend--invalidate this theory.

Far more compelling is the connection solidified through the rigorous research of the late Frank Andrejasich of Summit, Illinois, which matches the legendary lady to a wholly different entity. In August 1994, Andrejasich's brother mailed him an article which mentioned the Southwest Side's most famous phantom. Already familiar with the story, Frank became swiftly smitten with the tale, finding that a number of his fellow parishioners at Summit's St. Joseph Catholic Church had more than a nodding acquaintance with the local legend.

In assembling his impressive dossier on the elusive Mary, Andrejasich accumulated many opinions on the phantom's earthly identity. Relying heavily on the recollections of his cousin, Mary Nagode, and the keen memory of John Poljack, Sr., a Slovenian emigrant, retired Prudential insurance manager and St. Joseph parishioner, Frank waded through a variety of first and second-hand accounts, newspaper articles, burial records and photographs. He was astounded by the prominence of the legend in local lore and fascinated by the ability of so many individuals, including a number of his fellow parishioners, to place Mary in their own experience.

One of these, the late Chester "Jake" Palus, turned out to be the younger brother of our Jerry Palus, supposed to have been Mary's first dance partner in 1936. According to Jake, Jerry had been the passenger in his friend's car when the pair took "Mary" home that remarkable night, and she disappeared en route to the address she had given as her home. Though he recites the story with ease, Jake himself has no comment on his brother's tale, refusing to express either credulity or disbelief.

Claire and Mark Rudnicki-friends, neighbors, and former St. Joseph parishioners-told Andrejasich that Resurrection Mary could be traced to the 1940s, when a young Polish girl crashed near Resurrection Cemetery at around 1 :20 a.m., after she took the family car to visit her boyfriend in Willow Springs. According to this version of the story, the girl was buried in a term grave at Resurrection. Appropriately, Andrejasich wonders why a couple that was well off enough to own a car in the 1940s would need to bury their daughter in a term grave. Adding to the explanations is another parishioner, Ray Van Ort, who tells how he and his bride-to-be were the first witnesses at the scene of an accident on Archer in 1936, when a black Model A sedan collided with a wide-bed farm truck at 1:30 a.m. According to Van Ort, of the two couples in the car, only one person survived, a girl who was badly hurt. Both men and another girl perished. Today, Van Ort is convinced that this was the accident that killed our would-be Resurrection Mary. Still another parishioner claims that the wayward wraith was, in life, Mary Miskowski of the southside Chicago neighborhood of Bridgeport. In this narrative, Miskowski was killed crossing the street in late October in the 1930s, on her way to a Halloween party.

After pondering the variety of accounts, combing early editions of the local papers, and checking with funeral directors and cemetery managers, Andrejasich came to believe that the ghost known as Resurrection Mary is the spiritual counterpart of the youngest of all the candidates: a12-year-old girl named, surprisingly, Anna Norkus.

Born in Cicero, Illinois in 1914, Norkus was given the name of Ona, Lithuanian for Anne. In that era, it was not the custom for Lithuanian immigrants to christen infants with two names. But after 1918, children were baptized with a Christian name and an historic name to further pride in their main country. As a young girl, Anna's devotion to the Blessed Mother led her to begin using the name Marija, Mary, as her middle name. By the time she neared her teenage years, Anna had grown into a vivacious girl. Blonde and slim, she loved to dance, and it was her relentless begging that convinced her father, August, Sr., to take her to a dancehall for her 13th birthday. On the evening of July 20, 1927, father and daughter set out from their Chicago home at 5421 S. Neva for the famous Oh Henry Ballroom, accompanied by August's friend, William Weisner, and Weisner's date. I won't go into everything that happened that night (which apparently included the revelers leaving the ballroom to bail someone out of jail), but at approximately 1 :30 a.m., the travelers passed Resurrection Cemetery via Archer Avenue, turning east on 71st Street and then north on Harlem to 67th Street. There, the car careened and dropped into an unseen, 25-foot-deep railroad cut.

Anna was killed instantly.

After the accident, her father, August Norkus was subject to devastating verbal abuse, even being told that Anna's death had been God's punishment for allowing the girl to go dancing at such a young age. In reality, the blame rested with the Streets Department, who had failed to post warning signs at the site of the cut. In fact, another death, that of Adam Levinsky, occurred at the same site the night after Anna's demise.

Between July 28th and September 29th, an inquest was held at Sobiesk's Mortuary in adjacent Argo. Heading up the five sessions was Deputy Coroner Dedrich, the case reviewed by six jurors. The *Des Plaines Valley News* carried the story of the inquest. Mary Nagode described the sad procession that left the Norkus home on a certain Friday morning.

First in line was Anna's older sister Sophie, followed by her older brother August, Jr. The pastor, altar boys, and a four-piece brass band preceded the casket, borne on a flatbed wagon with pallbearers on each side. Relatives and friends followed the grim parade for three blocks to the doors of St. Joseph's in Summit, where Anna had made her First Communion only a year before. Between the band and the priest walked a terrified Mary Nagode, a friend of Anna's who had been pressed into service as a wreath-bearer. On summer vacation, Nagode was weeding on an asparagus farm in Willow Springs when she had a visitor. It was Gus Norkus, Anna's father or brother, asking her to participate in the funeral, since Mary had made her First Communion with Anna and owned a white dress. When Mary returned home that evening, her mother informed her that she had accepted the request on her behalf. The girl was deeply dismayed at the proposition. Mrs. Nagode reminded her daughter that refusal of such a request would be a sin against Roman Catholic moral living, which dictates that one must attend to the burial of the dead. Anna was scheduled for burial in one of three newly-purchased family lots at St. Casimir Cemetery, and it is here where Andrejasich found the "if" that may have led to an infamous afterlife for Anna as Resurrection Mary, or as Anna called herself, Marija.

Andrejasich discovered that at the time of Anna's death a man named Al Churas Jr., brother-in-law to Mary Nagode, lived across the road from the gates of Resurrection Cemetery, in a large brick bungalow that still stands today. Al's father was in charge of the gravediggers and was given the house to live in as part of his pay. In the mid-1920s, gravedigging was hard, manual labor, rewarded with low pay. Strikes were common. As Resurrection was one of the main Chicago cemeteries, the elder Churas was often sent to the cemeteries of striking gravediggers to secure the bodies of the unburied. Returning to Resurrection with a corpse in a wooden box, Churas' duty was to bury it temporarily until the strike ended and the body could be permanently interred in the proper lot. Because of poor coffin construction and the lack of refrigeration, a body could not be kept long, except in the ground. If the strike dragged on, identification at the time of relocation could be gruesomely difficult. Thus, reasoned Andrejasich, if the workers at St. Casimir were striking on that July morning in 1927, it is quite possible that young Anna Norkus was silently whisked to a temporary interment at Resurrection, and that a rapid decomposition rendered her unidentifiable at the time of exhumation. The result? A mislaid corpse and a most restless eternity, if only one is willing to believe.

Those not quite convinced may be persuaded otherwise by a further bit of Frank's musing, this time connecting the otherworldly Anna to the sneering specter seen on the road outside of her alleged resting place. The elder August Norkus followed his youngest child to St. Casimir 30 years after her death, a broken man besieged by alcohol and blamed to his grave for his daughter's demise. As Andrejasich reasons, it wouldn't take much else to make a ghost out of this ill-fated character. And yet, how much more there is (again, if only one believes in ghosts) if Anna was mistakenly buried away from her family. Has Resurrection Marija been combing the southwest suburbs for her father, this poor soul watching and waiting for his lost, beloved girl?

Just a handful of years ago, I received a Facebook message from a man who had recently moved to the Chicago area. He was a truck driver and had secured a job in the western suburbs where he could be home every night, as opposed to the long-distance hauls of which he had grown tired. He found a house off of Harlem Avenue, just before Archer Avenue turns into Archer Road, immediately north of the village of Summit. His commute each day began at 4am and took him south on Archer to his place of employment, and then back home in the early afternoon.

One morning, while making his way through Summit in the early morning darkness, he saw someone at the corner of a downtown intersection. As he neared the spot, he saw that it was a girl, blonde and fair, of what he thought to be about fourteen years old. She was dressed all in white—a white party dress, stockings and dress shoes—, and she wore a white headpiece of some sort with a veil attached. As he passed her, she looked at him and smiled. He told me he got the impression from her that she was a lot of fun to be around, that she would be a happy and uplifting presence in her family and to her friends.

It wasn't until he was some blocks further down Archer and passing Resurrection Cemetery that he realized it was a weekday morning and around 4 am. Yet he had seen this young girl, all alone, on a deserted street corner, and dressed as if ready for her First Communion. He mentioned that she had short, bobbed blonde hair and looked "like a young Gwyneth Paltrow."

He went back to see if she was ok, but by the time he arrived at the spot, she was gone.

When he contacted me, he knew nothing about Chicago history, let alone Chicago ghostlore, and he asked me, "Has anyone reported seeing a girl in a while dress there on Archer Avenue?"

I laughed and said, "Oh, yeah."

I sent him the photograph of Anna Norkus that Frank Andrejasich had given me so many years before. I told him about the legend of Resurrection Mary. And I told him about Anna's Communion dress.

#

Despite seemingly innumerable similar scenarios and the untiring work of devoted researchers like Frank Andrejasich, specialists in modern folklore have utterly disregarded local attempts to trace Resurrection Mary to any earthly counterpart. Instead, many scholars explain Mary as merely a localized version of the widespread vanishing hitchhiker legend. These legends have passed from generation to generation throughout history, but the 20th century versions always follow a strikingly similar pattern. A hitchhiker, usually a young woman, is either picked up along a dark road or met at a dance, from where she is given a ride home. In the latter situation, her would-be suitor may report having danced with the young woman, finding her somewhat cold. In both situations, she gives her escort vague directions to her house, but along the way she suddenly vanishes from the car. Sometimes, the driver will have procured her address and proceeds to the house to ask whether the girl has returned safely home. Upon his arrival, he is told that the girl, whom he recognizes in a photograph displayed in the home, was previously killed in a car accident on the road or near the dance hall where she met her unfortunate escort.

The Resurrection Mary stories do bear an uncanny resemblance to these widespread tales. In fact, accounts of Mary by eyewitnesses have conformed to the universal model even more perfectly than do most second-hand legends, suggesting that it may likely have been *this* enigma that inspired what is now a universal "campfire tale" or "urban legend." Indeed, the existence of so many first-hand reports raise questions about the assertions that Mary is mere folklore.

Reports of Resurrection Mary increased significantly during renovations of the cemetery in the mid-1970s. It was also around this time that the phantom began to become more animated. and adventuresome. In 1973, Mary is believed to have shown up at least twice in one month at a far Southwest-side dance club called Harlow's, 8058 S. Cicero Avenue, wearing a dress that looked like a faded wedding gown. A Harlow's manager described her as having "big spooly [sic] curls coming down from a high forehead. She was really pale, like she had powdered her face and body." Dancing alone in an off-the-wall fashion, she was as obvious as could be, yet, despite bouncers at the door who carded all guests, no one ever saw her come in or leave.[33]

That same year, at Chet's Melody Lounge, an annoyed cab driver bounded in asking about his fare, a young blonde woman. The manager gave him the only answer he had: "A blonde woman never came in here."[34] A number of years later, a driver happened to be passing the cemetery when he glimpsed a young woman standing on the other side

---

33 *Chicago Tribune* Oct 25, 1992
34 Cab driver. "a young woman never came in here." article

of the gates, clutching the bars. Worried that someone had been locked inside after closing, he hurried to report the incident to the local police, who hastened to rescue the reluctant prisoner. Upon their arrival, they found the cemetery deserted, but their inspection of the gates revealed a chilling spectacle: not only had two of the bars been pried apart, but the impressions of a pair of delicate hands remained, bearing witness to the feminine touch that had accomplished the task.

When cemetery management saw the state of the bars, they reportedly called in officials from the Archdiocese of Chicago, who allegedly removed the imprinted bars and whisked them away. Akin to stories of aliens in warehouses are local whisperings about the mysterious bars sitting today in some secret Archdiocesan storehouse. Not long after the removal of the damaged bars, embarrassed cemetery officials installed what they called "repaired" bars, insisting that the bent bars had been welded back to normal and not, as many asserted, replaced with new ones. Still, some cemetery workers maintain that the bars were bent by a crew member's truck backing into the gate; the handprints were left by a worker's glove when he attempted to heat the bars with a blowtorch and bend them back into shape. In response to that claim, local believers say: Yes, the cemetery tried to blowtorch and restore the bars, to eradicate evidence of the spectral handprints, which witnesses continue to describe as the well-defined fingers of a frail female.

Whatever the claims, the tale's undeniable fascination lies in viewing the cemetery gates even to this day, as two strips of discolored metal remain in the exact spot which once bore the mysterious handprints. In fact, and there seems to be no reason to doubt the rumor, it is said that this part of the gate refuses to "take" either primer or paint. The result? An embarrassing but apparently ineradicable scar on the face of the cemetery and its management.

As if this carnival weren't enough for the cemetery to bear, it was also around this time that Mary began to experiment with new methods. Folklorists have described a certain model of the phantom hitchhiker which is best termed the "spectral jaywalker," that is, the ghostly vision that walks or simply appears in front of a moving vehicle. One such story tells of a Justice police officer who called an ambulance after hitting a woman in a bloody white dress who was wandering the road in front of the cemetery. When the paramedics arrived on the scene, there was no trace of the distressed woman. The officer in question went on the nationally syndicated paranormal-themed television show, "That's Incredible!" and told of his experience. Before doing so, he was warned that he would be fired if he did. Notwithstanding the alleged threats, the officer told his story to network audiences and was, at least by local accounts, relieved of his duties.

After a bizarre decade that seemed to mark the climax of her restlessness, Mary was back to her old tricks. Yet she didn't seem quite her old self. In 1989, on a blustery January night, a cab driver picked up a desolate young woman outside the Old Willow Shopping Center. Despite the inclement weather, she wore a beautiful white party dress and patent leather dancing shoes. Climbing in the front seat, she made it clear that she needed to get home, motioning the driver up old Archer Avenue. But this time she behaved differently. She seemed confused, unable to give lucid answers to the cabby's polite questions. Finally, with all the clarity she could muster, the girl remarked, "The snow came early this year." Then, in front of a time-worn shack across the road from Resurrection, the disoriented passenger ordered, "Here!" and disappeared without another sound.

Also in the late 1980s, two teen-aged boys were driving along Archer Avenue at Christmastime when they saw a strange woman dancing down the road outside the cemetery fence. They noted that other passers-by seemed totally unaware of her antics; in fact, they didn't seem to see her at all. The teens reported the bizarre scene to their parents, who at once related the famous tale of Resurrection Mary. Never having heard the story before, the boys must have questioned whether the off-the-wall vision they had seen was really the same as the legendary hitchhiker, whose aloof sophistication seemed wholly unbefitting the wacky wayfarer of their own experience.

What has happened to Mary in these past decades? A ghost hunter's classic summation would point to the disruption of the Bregovy grave during cemetery renovations. Investigators might theorize that this disruption could have caused Mary's apparent disorientation. Possibly. For, although the site of the grave was finally disclosed to the public after many years of secrecy, the plot turned out to be unmarked. Mary Bregovy's was a "term grave," a plot that was sold on 25-year terms during the '20s and '30s, in a section of Resurrection that was renovated during the '60s and '70s. It is therefore possible that the girl's family either did not repurchase the grave, resulting in the filling-in of the plot, or that they or the cemetery administration moved the grave to discourage the curious.

There is one other peculiarity worth noting. Resurrection Mary has traditionally been connected with the former Oh Henry (Willowbrook) Ballroom, where she is alleged to have danced during her lifetime, and where she is guessed to have danced her last. Some accounts, however, specify that on the night of her death, Mary was at a dance for Christmas or even Advent, the Christian season preceding Christmas. The fact that so many Resurrection Mary encounters have occurred in December might seem to render this obscure lore somewhat more credible, although the timing would also undermine the connection to Mary Bregovy, who was killed on March 10th. Dealing only with conjecture about the behavior of ghosts, researchers continue to seek the Bregovy grave at Resurrection Cemetery in hopes of finding some end to a grueling but engaging search.

Whoever Resurrection Mary is, and whenever she may materialize, the apparent changes in this legend's "personality" continue to present a nagging appeal to the folklorists who have denied that Mary has any psychic reality, and who have accordingly classified her with other bizarre by-products of the oral tradition. Although I believe the 20th century tales of the Archer Avenue hitchhiker, I have long pointed out the similarities between these and the incident that occurred to musicians Looney and Kelly back at St. James Sag in the late 19th Century. The two ghost stories share a great number of specific elements, including the singular image of a woman in white, a cemetery, a vehicle, a dance hall and Archer Avenue itself.

Ultimately, regardless of the temptation to give in to folkloric categorization of Mary, the primary difficulty remains: a good number of first-hand accounts of these encounters have been recorded. In the case of urban legends like that of the vanishing hitchhiker, the incidents are supposed to have occurred to "a friend of a friend" or someone's "boyfriend's mother's friend" and so on. If we accept the first-hand accounts of this hitchhiker at face value, the phenomenon of Resurrection Mary continues to challenge the most skeptical observers, and to lure the most hopeful believers to her stomping grounds.

Susan Stursberg was one of the latter who decided to try her luck at spotting the famed and filmy form. Her account is unique in this author's experience, and deserves retelling:

I was out with a friend one night who had just bought a new car. I had not been to Archer Avenue and was itching to go, so we decided to take a drive. First, we stopped to see her boyfriend who was playing in a band at a nearby suburban bar. We said hi, told him we were going for a drive but did not tell him where. So we proceeded to Chet's Melody Lounge, talked to the regulars, played "The Ballad of Resurrection Mary" on the jukebox and some pool. We left in a couple of hours when 2 a.m. rolled around, drove to the cemetery gates, parked and peered in, seeing the repaired gates and getting a good case of the creeps. On the way home we joked about giving Mary a ride in the new car. Later that night my friend, Kristin, dropped me off at my apartment and went home to hers.

As her boyfriend, Mike, heard the car pull up he peeked out the window, then not wanting to appear worried and waiting up he dropped the shade. Kristin let herself in and closed the door. Mike asked, "Where's Susan?" Kristen told him that she dropped me off first. He asked, "Well, who was in the car with you?" To this day he swears that when he looked out the window, he saw a pale face look back at him from the passenger's side of the front seat.

Despite such compelling accounts as this and those others detailed in these pages, the doubters stand fast. Among them are those extreme locals like Gail Ziemba, who lives across the road from Resurrection Cemetery. Easily summing up her 20 years' experience with the legendary ghost, Ziemba maintains: "I've never seen anything." In response, believers would remind her that only men are privileged to see Resurrection Mary, although there have been cases in which a man and a woman traveling together have both reported a glimpse or two of something.

And while neighbors like Ziemba continue to shake their heads at the legend, other neighbors of the cemetery have been pushed to reconsider their doubt. Early one morning in late summer of 1996, Chet Prusinski himself, owner of Chet's Melody Lounge, was backing out of his driveway when a man came rushing across the road, yelling that he needed a phone. He had hit a woman on Archer Avenue and couldn't find the body. Attesting to his claim was a truck driver who had been driving behind him. He, too, had witnessed the grisly incident and remained at the scene to testify on the woman's behalf. Prusinski agreed to call the police, but hastened to disengage himself from the whole affair, fearing that he would be accused of staging a publicity stunt for his bar. The "accident" was quietly resolved and little was made of the event. However, those who always take note, took note. And, of course, those who always laugh, laughed.

Yet even those Southwest-siders who discredit Resurrection Mary know that much of what makes their culture special is wrapped up in the folds of her legendary white dress. And because of this, she is, even to nonbelievers, a priceless treasure, just as she was to a fictionalized witness in Kenan Heise's novel, "something precious, whoever or whatever she is. To her, I say, 'God bless you.'"[35]

---

35 "to her I say, god bless you"-Kenan Heise

ABOUT THE AUTHOR

Ursula Bielski is the founder of Chicago Hauntings and the host of WYCC PBS's *The Hauntings of Chicago*.

An historian, author, and parapsychology enthusiast, she has been writing and lecturing about Chicago's supernatural folklore and the paranormal for nearly twenty years and is recognized as a leading authority on Chicago and Midwest ghostlore and cemetery history. Her tours are the basis and foundation of our Chicagoland routes.

www.ingramcontent.com/pod-product-compliance
Lightning Source LLC
LaVergne TN
LVHW022325080426
835508LV00013BA/1320